HOUSEHUSBANDS

Men and Housework in American Families

WILLIAM R. BEER

PRAEGER SPECIAL STUDIES • PRAEGER SCIENTIFIC
J.F. BERGIN PUBLISHERS

Library of Congress Cataloging in Publication Data

Beer, William R., 1943-
   Househusbands: men and housework in American families.

   Bibliography: p.
   Includes index.
   1. Househusbands—United States. I. Title.
HQ756.B43   1982   306.8′7   82-12079
ISBN 0-03-059978-4

Published in 1983 by Praeger Publishers
CBS Educational and Professional Publishing
A Division of CBS, Inc.
521 Fifth Avenue, New York, New York 10175 U.S.A.

3456789   056   98765432

Printed in the United States of America

To R.S.B., N.C.B., & J.S.B.

Contents

Contents

Foreword

What is "housework"? The word evokes the image of cooking, cleaning, child care, shopping, laundry and household maintenance. But what of mowing the lawn, trimming the hedges, weeding the garden, painting the house? What of taking care of the car, changing the oil and filter, washing and waxing the finish, tuning the engine? What of cutting firewood, repairing a bicycle, replacing a broken window pane? All are tasks that involve unsalaried work in a house or with its machines. Little objection would be raised to classifying the first six tasks as "housework." But to call the rest by this name would be highly controversial, because they are performed far more by men than by women. This is the key to understanding the conventional meaning of the term "housework": most often "housework" denotes tasks performed by housewives. In the United States men do immense amounts of housework, as in the jobs just mentioned, but neither they nor others refer to it as such.

The definition of "housework" is rooted in what social scientists call the sexual division of labor. One of the most universal facts of human social existence is the allocation of different jobs to men and women. In hunting and gathering societies, for instance, males generally do the hunting, while females generally perform child-rearing and other domestic functions. As societies become more complex, jobs continue to be assigned to males or females, but this is often arbitrary. The same activity, such as grinding grain, might in one society be exclusively masculine, while in another society might be exclusively feminine. Thus, although the sexual division of labor is nearly universal, there are few tasks that are universally masculine or feminine.

This is as true of housework in our society as it is of any other work. To say that cooking and child rearing are housework, but that cutting the grass and changing a tire are not, rests on the convention defining the first as part of a group of tasks that are exclusively female. Housework is, by common definition, women's work. Not that all women perform these jobs, but—except for unusual circumstances, such as life in the army or in times of sickness or separation—they are carried out by women. To say that this definition rests on social conventions, however, does not mean that its basis is flimsy or temporary. Social conventions, including the sexual division of labor, are more durable than such artifacts as cathedrals and cities, and far more durable than human beings themselves.

A study of men who do housework, then, is not a study of men who do unpaid work around the house, because there are millions of men in America who do a very great deal of such work. It is a study of men who do what is conventionally defined as women's work. Men who do housework are crossing one of the deepest and longest-standing barriers in human society, one that separates men's work from women's work. There have been mountains of books and articles published on the many women who have crossed this line, about their fears and hopes, the difficulties they encounter, the fulfillments and frustrations and ambivalences of doing work traditionally assigned to men. But practically nothing has been written about the experiences of men who go in the opposite direction. This report aims to correct that deficiency. It aims to find out about the experiences of men who do housework as it is commonly defined—cooking, cleaning, child care, shopping, laundry, and household maintenance.

What should we call such men? They are obviously not all that different from other men, except in their tasks around the house, so why call them anything at all? One reason is simply for brevity's sake; the phrase "men who do housework" is cumbersome. But there is a more important reason. Sooner or later, the roles that people play in society affect them. While at the beginning a social role may be simply an activity that people carry out because it is expected of them, after a while they come to expect these things of themselves. This is what sociologists call "internalization": roles become part of us. A man who does housework for a long period of time is very likely to think of himself differently as a result. This is another reason for calling such men by a particular term, because they probably have come to look at themselves and others in particular ways.

About fifteen years ago, news reports from Sweden began talking about the growing trend of the *hemmaman*, a term that can probably best be translated into English as "househusband." These reports referred to men whose wives worked outside the home while the men stayed at home to take care of household and children. At the time, this was regarded as another oddity from far-out Scandinavia. The term began to be used seriously by American social scientists after it was used by James Levine in a book published in 1976, *Who Will Raise the Children?* For Levine, the term refers to men who are like the *hemmaman*, whose families do things "the other way around." Sociologists refer to this as "role reversal," but whatever term is used, it refers to men who do the jobs usually assigned to housewives, while their wives do the work of providing that men traditionally do.

In the strictest definition of the term, then, househusbands do not work outside the home. But it seems logical to use the term with some modification to refer to men who do a substantial part of the housework in addition to working outside the home. After all, women who work outside the home are often said to have two jobs, that of housewife as well as their paid job. Why not refer to men who do a large proportion of the housework as equal-time househusbands?

The discussion of the term "housewife" by people who have reported on this role justifies this use of the term. Both Helen Z. Lopata and Ann Oakley say that a housewife is someone who is *responsible* for the upkeep of the home. A housewife does not even have to *do* the housework, according to these definitions, since she can supervise domestic help and still be a housewife. *Reponsibility* is what makes a housewife, even though husbands may "help out." The fact that the man's job is traditionally called "helping out" underlines whose responsibility "housework" traditionally is. So a man who does the dishes occasionally or who takes care of the children in emergencies can hardly be thought of as a househusband. However, when a man does 40 or 50 percent of the housework, it is obvious that he is doing more than helping out: that he has assumed much of the responsibility for housework. This is why in my study I refer to men who share substantially in the housework as equal-time househusbands. There are some men in the study who are full-time househusbands, but all deserve the term with one modifier or another.

Some might object that househusbands are not the same as housewives, in the sense that men cannot possibly be expected to behave the same as women, who, ever since they were little girls, have been trained to expect such responsibilities when they marry. This may be true, but we do not know it, and it is all the more reason to find out whether men feel differently about housework and, if so, how. A study of men who have the lifelong avocation of housework would be interesting but impossible, because such men do not exist. Instead, we are looking here at men who are adapting to a totally new and "inappropriate" set of jobs.

In Chapter 1, we look at the general topic of men's roles and how they are changing in American society, and then at some facts about househusbands from the few sources there are, noting how many there are, what they do around the house, and what contemporary public opinion is in this regard. This is followed by a brief description of my study of househusbands, stating how I went about gathering the information reported in the rest of the book. Chapter 2 deals with the question, "Why do men do housework?" It compares research done by others with the results of the present survey, and then looks at the accounts of the men themselves, regarding how their domestic division of labor came about. With some understanding of why men do housework, the next question is raised in Chapter 3: "Do men like housework?" This is not just a question of personal like or dislike, because men's feelings about housework have an important effect on their families. As I have remarked earlier, social roles have an inner effect on people as time goes by, and the questions dealt with in Chapter 4 are the effects of doing housework on men's feelings about themselves, their spouses, and work outside the home. Then, having discussed the main results of the study, we turn in Chapter 5 to consideration of why there are not more househusbands, and what measures might be taken to encourage men to be actively involved in family work. Chapter 6 concludes the book with a discussion of the future of the househusband in the American family. Appendix A provides a detailed description of the method used in this book; Appendix B, a facsimile of the questionnaire used.

The research for this book was supported by a grant from the City University of New York PSC-CUNY Research Award Program. I would like to express my appreciation for this support.

My research assistant for the project, Mr. Joshua Sky, was precise, reliable, and thorough. Many of the good aspects of this study are due to the high quality of his work; its drawbacks are my fault and mine alone. I would also like to thank the staff of the South Huntington Public Library for the many ways in which they assisted me in this work. The staff of the New York Public Library were also extremely helpful. Finally, I would like to express my gratitude to four successive chairmen of the Department of Sociology at Brooklyn College—Prof. Sidney Aronson, Prof. Paul Montagna, Prof. Daniel Claster and Prof. Jerome Krase—for having granted me enough released time to carry this project through to the end.

Preface

A mid-autumn Thursday, so I am on child-care duty, and Rose sleeps while I get up with Nicole. It is 6:30 in the morning and a bright, clear day outside. In her crib, Nicole is stirring and gurgling. When my face peers over the railing, I get a smile. I lift her up, cradling her head out of reflex, even though she doesn't need it any more. I hold her in my arms for a minute and give her a kiss and a hello. Then I lay her down on her changing table, and remember to put the strap over her stomach so that she cannot fall off if I have to turn away. Unzipping her stretch suit, I deftly ease out her little legs and remove the soiled Pamper. It strikes me for the hundredth time that whoever invented Pampers should be classed with whoever invented the wheel and peanut butter: they are so convenient! The used one plops into a plastic garbage bag, and I use a Wet One to clean Nicole's bottom. Flip out a fresh Pamper, lay it open under her. Now comes the Desitin. You have to put it on because it gives sure-fire protection against diaper rash. But it is made with cod-liver oil, which leaves a smell on my fingers that I loathe. Odd, it's the only part of changing diapers that I don't like. Pull up the front panel, tuck the corners around her hips and seal with the adhesive strips. There, clean and fresh. Now, off with the stretch suit and undershirt. Pause to tickle her tummy and kiss her feet. Her arms and legs wave frantically, and she giggles. Maybe it's my moustache that makes her laugh. Fresh undershirt, fresh stretch suit. It's a delicate job getting them on, because she hasn't learned to keep her limbs stiff to get them into a sleeve. Then she's tidy and neat and ready for some breakfast. Carry her into the kitchen tucked into the crook of my left elbow, pausing to chuck dirty clothes into laundry chute with my right hand. Boy, am I getting efficient. Into her infant seat on top of the table, so I have easy access while I'm sitting down. Run the tap water until it's very hot, put the sterilized bottle full of milk into a pot partly filled with hot water. Talking to her the whole time, part words, part sounds, mostly singing. Plug in the coffee that Rose thoughtfully set up the night before, so it brews while I'm feeding Nicole. I get out the jars of apricot and oatmeal. If I had more time, I'd have made my own oatmeal, but occasionally prepacked baby food makes infant care so much easier that it is very tempting: just open the jar, scoop out the food, and throw away the used container. After she's eaten half of each jar, they go in the fridge, and she's ready for the bottle. Lying in the crook of my left arm, next to my heart, she drinks her bottle. The technology of bottle feeding allows Rose the freedom to pursue her career, and me to be included in this form of close and sensual communication. The towel goes over my right shoulder when she's finished, and she burps away with her chin resting on it. Afterward, she goes in her playpen and I get half an hour or so with my coffee and breakfast and the *New York Times.* Rose gets up and we share the paper. Then I have a while to work at my desk in my study while Rose plays with the baby and gets ready to go to school. A feeding for Nicole at ten o'clock, change diapers again, and then put her in for a nap. I can put in two solid hours at work before she wakes up and it's time to change her again. I get much more work done when the time is limited like this, because I don't fool around. I make a sandwich for myself and eat it before she eats, and then play with her for a while after lunch. Put her in her playpen and try to read, but as she grows up she's getting more and more interested in things outside and often pushes herself up on her arms and looks around, calling me. Perhaps we go for a walk through the falling maple leaves on our block, with her riding in a pack on my back. Put her in for another nap after feeding around two, and then wash and wax the kitchen floor while she's sleeping. The only part I don't like is trying to get off the old wax with ammonia. I used to get down on my hands and knees and put the wax on with a rag, but now I use a sponge mop, which isn't as careful but is a lot more pleasant. After Nicole wakes up, Kristi, an older girl from the neighborhood, often comes over to play with her. Kristi and Nicole love each other, and Kristi will only occasionally accept any money for playing with Nicole. I get on my running clothes and put in five or six miles while they play and the early autumn evening falls. Once I am home, hamburgers grill while I shower quickly. Maybe I wait until after dinner to take a bath with Nicky. At suppertime, I read her a story. After we are finished, the dishes go in the dishwasher, and the counters and tabletop get a wash. Then the two of us cuddle on the bed while I watch the news on television. Soon it is time for her to go to bed. I change her again and put on a double diaper, a trick we learned to keep things dry during the night. Then a song with her in my arms and she goes to bed. Start the dryer if I've done laundry, and fold clothes. Usually after a day of work in my study, child care, cooking, cleaning, and running, I'm too tired to work after supper, so I either watch television or read a novel until Rose gets home around 10:30. She is so tired from teaching graduate courses for four hours straight that she collapses, and I'm not far behind.

My wife and I had both had jobs while we shared an apartment in Brooklyn. It seemed natural that we share the household tasks, particularly since it had been my apartment before she came to stay. These tasks are fairly minimal for a couple without children in a small place. There were not many dishes to wash: breakfast was a hasty affair, and we ate lunch on the job and ate out in the evening about once a week. Laundry wasn't much of a problem, and unless we entertained nonstop the apartment only needed cleaning about once a week. We are both nonsmokers, too, so there weren't even any ash trays to empty. Even though housework was light, we shared it pretty much equally.

When we decided to start a family, I was eager to be involved in the whole prenatal process as well as in the delivery of the baby itself. I do not really understand why I was so excited. I was not consciously responding to any part of my own upbringing, and my previous experiences with children did not make me wild about them, even though I had never regarded them with stereotypical male indifference. I only know that when the prospect of being a father became real rather than potential, some deep feeling was aroused in me whose existence I had never suspected. We attended a prenatal clinic, so that even though I was not carrying the baby, I felt that I was as involved in being pregnant as it is possible for a man to be. At the urging of the midwives who taught the program, we came to think of ourselves as a team working together during a long and difficult delivery, and although I wasn't as tired as Rose when our daughter made her first cries of life, I was by far the more openly emotional. As a father, I felt like an active participant, and I was glad not to be one of those poor nervous wrecks pacing around a waiting room waiting for news.

Because I had a strong role in the birth of our daughter, it was fairly automatic that I play just as strong a part in taking care of her. For us, starting a family coincided with moving to a house in the suburbs, and with Rose starting a new teaching job. Within six weeks of these changes, we started a schedule that we have had pretty much ever since. I teach on Mondays, Wednesdays and Fridays, while Rose teaches on Tuesdays and Thursdays. When I am teaching, Rose takes care of our daughter, and when she is teaching I do the baby care. College teachers spend most of their time outside the classroom doing research and writing. Because it is always tempting to play with Nicole rather than do our research and writing, for several hours two or three days a week we used to leave her with a woman in the neighborhood who provides day-care service. As she got older, we sent her to nursery school two days a week, which accomplished the same thing in terms of time. At the beginning I did less child care on weekends because I was writing a book and had to spend Saturdays at the library. Weekend child care has varied since then, depending on what our professions have required. Sundays Rose always sleeps late, I get up with Nicole and make pancakes for everybody. I always put Nicole to bed and read her a story and sing her a song before she goes to sleep. Overall, I do about 40 percent of the child care.

As for cooking and cleaning, I do more dishwashing, vacuuming, and washing and waxing floors than cooking. This is because I am not an imaginative cook, and while I have bursts of creative passion with a wok, the family would eat hamburgers and Weaver's chicken all the time if the cooking were left entirely to me. Of course, I do all the cooking on Tuesdays and Thursdays. To keep the house clean, we tried having a cleaning lady take care of the house every two weeks. We found not only that it was expensive (fifty dollars per month), but that the quality of the work was not always very good. I took over the job of vacuuming and washing and waxing the floors once a week. It's a lot cheaper, and the only person I can blame for sloppy work is myself. Rose's cleaning territory is dusting and the bathroom, which she attacks once a week.

We are fortunate to have a washing machine and dryer, so that the job of keeping clothes clean is not a heavy burden. We consider this a task for both of us, though Rose probably does more, as she is home more days per week than I. The only job that she does entirely is food shopping, once a week. I have suggested that I do more of it, particularly when I run out of something, but she says it's easier for her to do it all at once. The only housework that is mine alone is work in the yard—painting, repairing the house, shoveling snow, raking leaves, cutting grass, pruning bushes, cutting firewood, and splitting logs.

Of course, it was not all harmony. There were adjustments to make, but not the ones I had expected, such as being bothered at not being able to pick up and go out to a movie or take a trip. We both were ready to settle down, and felt little nostalgia for the mobility of childlessness. The two most important sources of conflict were adjusting to each other's expectations regarding housework, and the problems of budgeting time.

My standards for a neat and clean house were lower than Rose's. When I was single, I was not excessively messy, but I thought little of leaving a dish in the sink overnight or leaving newspapers and books around the place. Part of this was because as a boy I was never asked to clean up after myself, either in my own room or in any other part of the house. Partly, also, I was not a particularly neat person. When I heard the first criticism of my standards of cleanliness, I was convinced that Rose was being dictatorial and overly demanding, if not a little compulsive. But after a while I came to appreciate the feeling of a house where everything was put away, the kitchen was clean, dishes washed, and countertops scrubbed. It soon got to the point where I myself could not relax after supper unless everything was squared away. I learned higher standards of housekeeping, and now keep myself to them almost automatically; but at first it was a real source of conflict.

More important by far were the problems of scheduling work. There is always a trade-off between time spent on housework and time spent on professional work. But the real problem was child care. I found Nicole so engrossing that I would gladly have spent a lot of my work time playing with her. With a wife who had her own professional responsibilities, her own household jobs, and her own needs for being with Nicole as a mother—not to mention the rare times when we could get together ourselves—the problem of budgeting and allotting time was and is a constant source of potential friction. Time has to be strictly divided up, and we carry these schedules around in our heads.

All in all, we share most housework fairly equally, although we do not do the same tasks all the time. There are only a few jobs that only one of us does, and the rest are thought of as common obligations. This situation evolved naturally rather than being the result of some conscious design. The sharing of housework is the direct counterpart of our both having careers and contributing to the income of the household. If either of us, for some reason, stopped working outside the home, the division of responsibility would certainly change.

Since I began doing housework on an equal basis, what has struck me is how easy it is. I do not mean that all of housework itself is easy; I mean that to take over tasks conventionally regarded as "women's work" was not as difficult a personal experience as I had expected. Much of the activity, literature, and rhetoric of the feminist movement over the past decade has focused on the difficulties women encounter—both inside themselves and in the world around them—in assuming roles ordinarily performed by men. "Consciousness-raising" is aimed at least as much at overcoming women's own resistance to being "liberated" as at coping with the hostile reactions of husbands, other men, and other women. I expected, then, that I would not only encounter curious, if not derisive, attention from other people, but that I would have difficulty personally adjusting to doing housework. This expectation was all the greater because I came from a home in which my father never did any housework, and I had never been obliged to do any either. With all the emphasis on "role models" and the supposedly dire impact of the schooling of the sexes in sex-segregated jobs, I should have undergone some sort of trauma in starting activities for which I had not been trained at all.

I was quite surprised, then, when not only did I not receive so much as a lifted eyebrow when wheeling a baby carriage down the middle of my street, but I found myself enjoying these new tasks far more than I had expected. Not that I enjoy every aspect of child care, cooking, and cleaning. A few things about child care are unpleasant, such as having to wake up at five in the morning when a little girl wants to play or taking care of a baby who can only cry because she can't tell you that her head hurts or she has a fever. But the whole experience made me curious about the experiences of other men who were taking over housework as I had done. I wondered how they felt about it, whether they found it as much of an adventure as I did, if they learned about themselves as much as I had. This led me to start the study whose results are reported in this book.

I realize, of course, that the situation I have described is far from common. While we are by no means rich, we are reasonably well-off, and fit squarely into a middle-class tax bracket. Thus, we have gadgets that poorer people cannot afford. What is most uncommon about us is the fact that our jobs allow us great flexibility in work time. Teachers do not have more free time than anyone else, but they are not tied to a desk or an assembly line all day five days a week. One of the biggest obstacles to men's becoming more involved in housework is the inflexibility of their hours. This realization made me all the more curious about the reactions to housework among men whose scheduling problems are probably far more formidable than my own.

* * *

Stereotypes abound, and I feel compelled to make a few disclaimers before beginning. For a long time there was a popular belief that men were not involved in housework in any significant way, that they did not want to be, and that if they were, their nature would make them incompetent at the job. Men who did this work were seen as deviating from a norm of masculinity. But recently, as we will see later, information has come to light that these commonly held beliefs are too pat and simple to keep, and that in many ways they are simply wrong. On the other hand, many people interested in the roles of men and women in society are anxious to brand traditional men as evil oppressors; they argue that all sex-specific behavior, for men as well as for women, is restrictive, repressive, and downright bad. Similarly, many of the propagandists for "men's liberation" have encouraged men to redefine totally what masculinity means, to adopt feminine characteristics, to become both male and female, or androgynous. The "liberationists" have created their own stereotypes, and if a man is involved in innovating sex roles, he is commonly thought to be politically liberal, a feminist, hostile to traditional aspects of masculinity, and so on. None of these stereotypes is true, either in my case or in that of most of the men interviewed for this study.

I have never believed in the feminist stereotype of Western man as being incapable of expressing deep emotion, particularly for his fellow man. I was educated in the classics when I was a boy, and I remember too vividly the story of Achilles' friendship with Patroclus in Homer's *Iliad* to believe this. And probably the strongest image of a man in our civilization is that of a suffering and sensitive Christ, hardly a picture of rugged machismo. *Be a Man!*—Peter Stearns' excellent historical account of male roles in history—is a good antidote to half-baked generalizations about men in Western society.

Men can be good at housework, and the experience can often be a source of great personal and emotional satisfaction. At the same time, being involved in housework is not necessarily contradictory to manhood; a man does not have to become feminine to adapt. My own feeling is that doing housework makes me *more* of a man, because it is an adventure like others, with its tribulations and rewards. One of my hobbies is mountain climbing, and I have climbed all forty-six peaks over four thousand feet in the White Mountains of New Hampshire, as well as some peaks in the Rockies. A day of cooking, cleaning, child care and household management is not unlike climbing a mountain. Some of it is sweaty, gruelling work, but the pleasures, such as sunlight through the mist on Mount Washington, or seeing a toddler learn a new game, are constant enough to make it worth it. Sir Edmund Hillary, in response to the question why he climbed Mount Everest, responded, "Because it is there." Housework may not be Everest, but it is an adventure that awaits any man who wants to forge ahead and meet the challenges of unexplored territory.

HOUSEHUSBANDS

1 What Do We Know about Men and Housework?

In order to discuss the results of the survey of househusbands that forms the major part of this book, we must first place it in the perspective of the general discussion of sex roles that has concerned sociologists for the last thirty years. The literature that comprises this discussion is extensive, but suffers from two basic weaknesses. The first is that it discusses a topic that is changing so rapidly that data and theorizing from one decade are far out of date during the next, making necessary a constant reworking of our thinking about sex roles. The second weakness is that much of the discussion of sex roles is carried on from a partisan point of view, so that research is carried on, information is presented, and conclusions are drawn in order to make a polemical point. The result is that much of the literature on changing sex roles is of very limited use for those trying to learn how things are rather than how they should or might be.

In the first part of this chapter, we will try to ascertain how sex roles have been changing, both in terms of how people act and how they think. Next, we will examine what we know about the extent to which men share in household tasks in the United States. Because the subject of men and family work has been generally neglected, and because the people who are interested in it rarely do empirical studies, the facts and figures to be discussed are relatively few. This review of what we already know about househusbands sets the stage for a brief description of how the survey was conducted and an introduction to the general characteristics of the men who were interviewed.

CHANGING SEX ROLES IN THE UNITED STATES

Any discussion of men and housework in American families must acknowledge the larger context of sex roles in the American family and how they are changing. What follows is not meant to be an exhaustive discussion of the subject of sex roles and the modern nuclear family; the literature on that subject is vast. The discussion of househusbands, though, requires an overview of sex roles in the nuclear family in the United States and how sex roles have been changing over the last three decades.

All societies have a division of labor by sex. The most important institution in which this division of labor is both present and taught is the family. The family is the most basic social institution, because without it we could not survive as organisms; born helpless, all humans require some group not only to help them to cope with the social and physical environment but to teach them to cope by themselves. Thus, the sexual division of labor in the family is important in two essential ways, in that it both allots tasks within that group, which perpetuates the human race, and at the same time teaches young males and females the sorts of behaviors appropriate to their sex.

Two key terms used by social scientists in referring to the sexual division of labor in the nuclear family in the United States are *instrumental*, referring to the characteristics of male roles, and *expressive*, referring to those of female roles. In the words of the formulator of these terms:

> The *man* takes the more *instrumental* role, the *woman* the more *expressive*.... The area of instrumental function concerns relations of the system to the situation outside the system, to the meeting the adaptive conditions of its maintenance and instrumentally establishing the desired relations to external goal objects.... The expressive area concerns the "internal" affairs of the system, the maintenance of its integrative relations between the members, and regulation of the patterns and tension levels of its component units. [Parsons and Bales, 1955:23, 46-47.]

In other words, the male's orientation is outside the family: he is the representative of the family to the society at large and at the same time the member of the family with greatest responsibility outside it. The woman's role is that of maintaining the stability of the family, primarily by providing emotional support for all members of the family and providing an emotionally mediating function between family members. In different terms, the instrumental role is that of the breadwinner and the expressive role that of peacemaker.

Parsons is describing patterns within the nuclear family; these are only tendencies, and are by no means intended to be blueprints for the organization of family life, nor do these terms describe the "correct" role for men and women in all American families. The terms describe behavior that recurs in the organization of American families: they suggest the shape of the sexual division of labor in this context. Parsons was well aware of the wide variations from these norms that appear in actual American families, and was also aware that they were changing before his eyes. Although certain aspects of the instrumental and expressive dimensions of male and female familial roles are still very much with us, there is no question that sex roles have changed a great deal since the end of the Second World War.

In an article written over thirty years ago, Sirjamaki (1948) pointed out that roles in the American family were changing although the image of a strict division of labor between the sexes still prevailed, and observed that the role changes under way were difficult for both sexes.

> Women are...caught in a process of social change, in which the cultural configuration restrains them to traditional roles, while new ones are proffered by economic and social forces... Men, it must be pointed out, suffer in the realignment of roles, since they as much as women are conditioned to the status quo and may find it hard to accommodate themselves to change. [Pp. 469-70.]

The *status*, it is now known, is no longer *quo*, but relatively little is known about how men have reacted to the change, particularly in the area of the division of domestic labor. In the 1950s, Hacker (1957) recognized that whereas men's roles had changed considerably in the recent past, there was little adequate study of these changes and their consequences. She saw that there was little clarity either in what men expected of themselves or in what others expected of them. Around the same time, a study by Hurwitz (1960) showed that wives tended to have a much clearer idea of their roles in marriage than did their husbands. Even before the feminist movement of the 1970s, changing sex roles in American society meant uncertainty for men.

One of the most dramatic changes has been the increasing acceptance of women taking over roles that were traditionally regarded as appropriate only to men. Survey data published in *Public Opinion Magazine* (December 1979-January 1980) give a picture of how attitudes have changed regarding wives' employment outside the home. In 1938, only one out of five Americans believed that it was acceptable for a married woman to work outside the home. By 1945 approval had only increased to one American out of four, a surprisingly low figure in light of women's large-scale participation in the work force during the years of World War II. Over the next twenty-five years, those who approved of married women working rose to 60 percent, and by 1978 as many as 72 percent approved. Overall, these figures show clearly that, even as Sirjamaki and Parsons were making their observations, a rapid change in sex roles was under way, at least as far as women were concerned.

What of changes in opinion regarding behavior appropriate to men? The data are not as exhaustive, but they indicate that no less drastic a shift regarding male sex roles has been under way. Consider the results of a pool published in *Public Opinion Magazine* (October-November 1979) that showed responses to the question, "People have different definitions of what makes a real man. For each of the qualities I am going to read to you, would you tell me whether you feel it is very important for a real man to have, somewhat important, or not at all important?" This question was asked in 1968 and in 1978, and striking differences appeared in the proportions of respondents who indicated qualities it was "very important" and "somewhat important" for a real man to have. Being "physically strong" was considered important by 52 percent in 1968, but this declined to 29 percent in 1978. "Being a good provider" was cited as important by 86 percent in 1968, but this had diminished to 67 percent a decade later. Being "good at managing money" went from 80 percent to 65 percent. And being "handy around the house" declined from 50 to 46 percent. In only ten years, some very perceptible changes took place in people's conceptions of what qualities were desired in a "real man." In all of the four areas cited, the percentages declined, but what is most interesting is the way in which they have declined. The category in which the least decline took place, "handy around the house," was the category that was the least "instrumental," i.e., that was least involved in mediating between the family and the world outside. "Being a good provider" is clearly instrumental in the sense in which Parsons means this term, and "good at managing money" similarly implies a function that links the family economy to the economy at large. Even being "physically strong" has an instrumental dimension to it, because one function of man's physical strength has been to protect one's wife and family from external aggressors.

In both the conceptions of desirable behavior for men and for women, then, dramatic changes are under way, and these can be precisely measured by the kinds of opinion data presented above. And yet "instrumentality" and "expressiveness" are not a thing of the past. Both men and women in the United States cling strongly to some very traditional ideas of sex roles. A survey reported in *Public Opinion Magazine* (August-September 1981) provides evidence of this. Men and women were asked, "Suppose both a husband and wife work at good and interesting jobs, and the husband is offered a very good job in another city. Assuming they have no children, which one of these solutions do you think they should seriously consider?" Three alternatives were offered the respondents: "Wife should quit her job, relocate with her husband, and try to get another job in the new place"; "Husband should turn down the job and stay where they are so the wife can continue with her job"; "Husband should take the new job and move there; wife should keep her job and stay where she is; they should get together whenever they can on weekends, holidays and vacations." The first alternative can be considered the most "traditional," the second and third, egalitarian, with the third more so than the second. Very few men and women, 4 percent of each, accepted the third choice. A large majority of women, 85 percent, believe that a wife should quit her job and go with her husband. Only a small percentage of women, 11 percent, believe that a husband should give up the opportunity for a better job for the sake of his wife's career. What is particularly striking about the survey results is that fewer men (76 percent) than women supported the "traditional" choice, and that more men (20 percent) than women believe that a man should give up an opportunity for the sake of his wife's career. These figures show that, far from being hostile—at least in theory—to women's career opportunities, men are more in favor of accommodating them than women. Overall, both are very strongly in favor of retention of some traditional aspects of women's roles.

Finally, some public opinion data show that whereas there is a persistence in the "instrumentality" expected of the American man in terms of earning a living for his family, there are other ways in which American men are expected to be quite "expressive," far more than we might expect from Parsons' theorizing.

Another survey reported in *Public Opinion Magazine* (December 1979-January 1980) indicates what percentages of respondents—both male and female—believed certain types of behavior were important for men and women. "Spends time with children" was thought of as important for a man by 86 percent of the respondents, compared to 90 percent who thought it was an important attribute for a woman. "A good provider" was thought to be an important quality for a man by 82 percent, but only 42 percent thought it was important that a woman have this quality. Almost the same percentages thought it was important for a man (73 percent) and a woman (76 percent) to "put family above anything else." And the proportions who thought being a "good parent" was important for men and for women were almost the same, 86 percent and 89 percent respectively.

Perhaps the first observation that springs from these figures is the contrast between the 82 percent of these respondents who thought that being a good provider is a "very important quality for a man," and the 67 percent of the respondents discussed above who think that being a good provider is an important quality for a "real man" to have. There is not necessarily a contradiction between the findings. Many people may not feel that it is very important for a man to be a "real man." But the disparities between these figures illustrate that public opinion data should be read carefully and skeptically.

The variations within the poll results, however, are not so ambiguous. It is clear that the sample interviewed sees being a good provider as literally twice as important a quality for a man as for a woman. Particularly interesting is the expectation of expressive qualities important to a man: men are supposed to "spend time with children" almost as much as their wives, and the same expectation can be seen with regard to being "a good parent." In short, the traditional expectations that men are supposed to mediate between their families and the outside world are still there, albeit in somewhat attenuated form. But added to this is an expectation of expressiveness, a quality only newly required of men in the history of American sex roles.

Telling evidence of the overlapping of sex roles with regard to housework appears in another poll reported in *Public Opinion Magazine* (December 1979-January 1980). People were asked, "what kind of marriage do you think is the more satisfying way of life: one where the husband provides for the family and the wife takes care of the children, or one where the husband and wife both have jobs, both do housework, and both take care of the children?" The first alternative was endorsed by only 43 percent of the people interviewed, compared to 49 percent who chose the second (9 percent said both or neither or had no opinion). The results of this poll show how far people's expectations today differ from the opposites of instrumental and expressive roles that Parsons talks about. Although a very large minority of public opinion supports that view of the sexual division of labor as desirable, an even larger minority, the largest proportion of respondents, say that they think that a marriage is most satisfying when both the man and the woman carry out instrumental and expressive tasks.

This short discussion of changing sex roles in the American family leads us to the conclusion that sex roles are rapidly changing, but that is commonly known. Not so commonly known are the ways in which they are changing. Further, it is commonly recognized that women's participation in work outside the home, even in areas traditionally reserved for men, is becoming increasingly accepted, if not expected; at the same time, there is persistence of the "expressiveness" required of women, resulting in the well-known and exhaustively discussed conflicts between motherhood and career. Again, it is less commonly realized that a similar pattern has developed for male sex roles as well. Men are still required, by convention and law, to support their families and women are exempted from this. But at the same time, they are increasingly expected by themselves, as well as by others, to be willing and able to fulfill functions traditionally restricted to women. In addition to the well-known conflicts between career and family that women are undergoing, the same kinds of strains are occurring among men.

Very little is known about the psychological and social effects of these strains upon men. The present study has as its purpose the partial filling of this large gap in our knowledge of changing sex roles.

FACTS AND FIGURES ABOUT HOUSEHUSBANDS

Research on participation by American husbands in housework is meager; it includes statistics to be gleaned from census reports, sociological studies on the American division of domestic labor, and some other very recent works.

Census Data: Full-Time Househusbands

Census data are useful only for studying men who, because of "home responsibilities," are outside the labor force that is, men whose primary responsibilities are jobs in the home. The number of such men, i.e., full-time househusbands, is small. However, it is growing rapidly. In 1950 the number of men listed by the census as outside the labor force because they were "keeping house" was 81,000 whereas in 1971 it was 296,000, an increase of 265 percent. (U.S. Bureau of the Census, 1971:910.)

In another census report, the number of men not in the labor force because of "home responsibilities" increased from 221,000 in 1970 to 244,000 in 1976. Of these, whites went from 185,000 to 211,000, while non-whites decreased from 36,000 to 33,000. (U.S. Bureau of the Census, 1977, Table 631, p. 390.) These figures are not exactly the same as those cited earlier regarding "keeping house" because of the differences in the wording of the questions asked by the census. Between 1970 and 1976 the number of white full-time househusbands increased by about 14 percent, while the number of nonwhite househusbands decreased by 8.3 percent. This strongly suggests that the reasons for white men becoming househusbands are different from those for nonwhite men. The present study focuses exclusively on white househusbands; for an explanation of this procedure, see Appendix A. A systematic study of nonwhite househusbands remains to be done.

In summary, the census data indicate that married men are

nearly always employed outside the home, and are seldom involved full time in housework. What of men who work outside the home but who also do housework? For this information, we must turn to more refined data than are available from the Census Bureau.

The Division of Labor in the Home: General Characteristics

The most striking impression that appears in studies of the division of labor in American homes is that it varies a great deal from one household to another. For instance, a decade ago Campbell (1970) reported that there was great variety in the division of labor in the home, and that much of the variation was due to factors such as the size of the family, the amount of time between marriage and the birth of the first child, and the amount of time between births of children. This study showed that there is a tendency for men to do "instrumental" jobs, such as handling money and bills, whereas there is a tendency for women to do "expressive" jobs, such as putting children to bed. However, there is great variety in how different households divide up the tasks. Campbell found that "traditional boundaries are again crossed as...increased activity (as a result of the birth of a second child) involves such tasks as grocery shopping, evening dishes and child care." (Campbell, 1970:52.)

In one of the best-known studies of women and housework, Helen Lopata (1971) reported that in the sample interviewed, only 22 percent of housewives do all of the cooking in their homes with no help from their husbands. Ten percent of these women are regularly helped by the husbands, and 28 percent receive help in emergencies; in the latter group, seven percent of the husbands provide help and 19 percent take over completely. "All in all," this researcher found, "41 percent of the husbands help their wives with cooking in some way." In household cleaning, too, men often participate, with 39 percent of the respondent housewives reporting some assistance from their spouses, 11 percent saying that this participation is normal, and 18 percent saying that it occurs in emergencies. Similarly, the husbands helped 39 percent of the respondents with laundry, but 19 percent of these did so only in emergencies. In shopping, 64 percent of the women interviewed said that their husbands helped to some extent. "In all, two-thirds of the men of the family assist in making the purchases needed to run the house, and only 27 percent of the women carry on this function by themselves." An area where husbands' participation is equally great is in the area of child care, particularly when the children are youngest and need the most attention: "...66 percent of...[husbands] who have young children needing care assist in the process.... Fourteen percent of the fathers help always, but 10 percent only contribute during emergencies." (Lopata, 1971:113-20.)

Besides sociologists, advertising agencies are quick to perceive trends such as the growth of househusbanding in the United States, and market research is another area that yields information. For instance, Cunningham and Walsh, Inc., published a report in 1980, "Husbands as Homemakers," which gives a picture of the division of labor in the American family. Their study was based on a national probability sample of married men, so that it is more representative than the other studies of time spent by men on housework that have so far been discussed.

According to this survey, 77 percent of American men "ever do grocery shopping," 70 percent "ever cook," 44 percent "prepare complete meals," 47 percent vacuum, 41 percent wash dishes, 37 percent make beds, and 33 percent do laundry (Cunningham & Walsh, Inc., 1980: appendix, Table 1). On the basis of this evidence, we would have to conclude that the participation of American married men in housework is extensive. "Ever do grocery shopping" and "ever cook" are categories that the study was particularly interested in, because it aimed to find consumer patterns among men. The three categories, "prepare complete meals," "vacuum," and "wash dishes" are perhaps most instructive for our purposes, because, aside from child care, they represent the bulk of the routine tasks that must be carried out in a household. And the results of the study show that in all of them, over 40 percent of American men carry out these tasks, although it is not clear what percentage of the time required by the task is carried out by the men interviewed. This same study looks at variations in the domestic division of labor in different income and age groups; these results will be discussed at greater length in Chapter 2.

The Cunningham and Walsh results are corroborated by another representative study of 452 married men done by a different advertising agency. Benton and Bowles, Inc. (1980) found that in their sample, 74 percent of the men took out the garbage, 66 percent shopped for extra food, and 53 percent washed dishes. In addition to these tasks, the researchers found that, in a two-week period, 80 percent of the men took care of the children (in households where the children were under 12 years of age,) 47 percent helped to cook a family meal, 39 percent vacuumed the house, 33 percent cooked an entire meal for the family, 32 percent did the main food shopping, and 29 percent did the laundry.

One other observation made by the Cunningham and Walsh report is worth including here. The question was, "Who pays the bills?" and the responses corroborate the conclusion that an overlapping of instrumental and expressive roles has taken place in the American family. Half of the respondents said that the wife performs this key instrumental role, mediating between the family and the outside social system by paying money that is owed, 25 percent said that the husband pays the bills, 23 percent said that both did so, while 2 percent did not respond (Cunningham & Walsh, Inc., 1980: Appendix, Table 21). Thus, in only one quarter of the families is the "traditional" arrangement present. This evidence reinforces the data discussed above, indicating that the sexual division of labor in the American home has changed drastically, and that men and women, in many American homes, share tasks once segregated by sex, while women have taken over many jobs once restricted to men.

So far, we have seen ample evidence that sex roles in the American family are changing, and changing rapidly. In addition to the well-known stresses for women caused by the contradictions between the demands of career and family, we have seen that similar stresses are being imposed on American men. However, the latter stresses have scarcely been recognized, let alone studied. We have also seen some general figures showing that men's participation in work conventionally considered women's work is far more common than is generally believed. Although the image of the nuclear family, with a strict division of labor between men in provider and instrumental roles and women in homemaker and expressive roles, is common among both its partisans and its enemies, nowadays this is more stereotype than reality, as Sussman and Cogswell (1972) suggest. They estimate that only about 35 percent of the households in America really conform to this pattern. Because of this, much writing about sex roles in the family is misinformed, and there are large gaps in our knowledge of the effects of variant family structures on men, women, and children. The principal aim of the present study is to fill the gap in our understanding of the effects these sex-role changes are having on men.

We turn now to brief descriptions of the method used in the study and of the sample of men who were interviewed.

THE HOUSEHUSBANDS SURVEY

Method

The principal tool used in this study was a survey of equal-time and full-time househusbands carried out in the New York area during 1979 and 1980. Fifty-six men were interviewed in depth, using a questionnaire composed of 55 questions ascertaining information about basic items such as birth data, occupation, number of children, and whether or not the respondent's spouse worked outside the home, as well as in-depth questions about why the respondent took over the housework, whether he liked it, and what effects he thought it had on him and his relationships. For reasons explained in Appendix A, the men interviewed were all white, American-born, and living with or married to a woman in a household, with at least one child present. The result of these interviews is a body of information about a selected sample of househusbands that includes recorded and transcribed accounts as well as data subject to statistical analysis. In the chapters that follow, we will be looking at the respondents' statements, assessing their meaning, and analyzing the relations between variables revealed by the aggregate data of the survey. In other words, this is both a qualitative and a quantitative study of househusbands. (For a detailed explanation of the method used, see Appendix A.)

Sample

The sample was designed not to be statistically representative but to test our assumptions about men and housework in a fairly homogeneous group of men. In spite of the (intended) homogeneity, these men differ considerably: age, occupation, education, religion, number of children, whether their wives are employed outside the home or not, amount of housework they do, and length of time they have been doing it. In terms of age, the sample includes a disproportionate number of men in their thirties (over two-thirds of the total): 4 are between the ages of 20 and 29 (7.1 percent), 39 are between the ages of 30 and 39 (69.6 percent), 5 are between the ages of 40 and 49 (8.9 percent) and 8 are between the ages of 50 and 59 (14.3 percent). The sample is also biased toward professional and managerial occupations (almost three-fourths of the total): 24 are in professional and technical jobs (42.9 percent), 17 are in managerial jobs (30.4 percent), 6 are in clerical jobs (10.7 percent), 4 are in service jobs (7.1 percent), 2 are skilled workers (3.6 percent), and 3 are in other kinds of jobs (5.4 percent). The sample tends to be well educated, too: 3 have a high-school education or less (5.4 percent), 11 have some college education (19.6 percent), 12 have a college degree (21.4 percent), 5 have a technical degree (8.9 percent), 18 have a master's degree (32.1 percent), and 7 have a professional degree such as a Ph.D. or a law degree (12.5 percent). There are 11 Catholics (19.6 percent), 23 Jews (41.1 percent), 5 Protestants (8.9 percent), and 17 who cited no religion or one other than the three listed above (30.4 percent). None of the sample has more than three children: 27 have one child (48.2 percent), 21 have two children (37.5 percent), and 8 have three children (14.3 percent). More than two-thirds of the wives are employed outside the home: 38 wives (67.8 percent), compared with 18 wives (32.2 percent) who are not employed outside the home. The proportion of housework reportedly performed by the respondents ranged from less than 30 percent to over 70 percent: 6 do between 20 and 29 percent of the houework (10.7 percent), 11 do between 30 and 39 percent of the housework (19.6 percent), 21 do between 40 and 49 percent of the housework (37.5 percent), 9 do between 50 and 59 percent of the housework (16.1 percent), 6 do between 60 and 69 percent of the housework (10.7 percent), and

3 do between 70 and 79 percent of the housework (5.4 percent). Most of the men have been doing housework for a fairly long period of time: 2 have been doing it for a year or less (3.6 percent), 2 for two years (3.6 percent), 5 for three years (8.9 percent), 4 for four years (7.1 percent), and 43 for more than four years (76.8 percent).

In summary, the sample tends toward men in their thirties, who are likely to be in professional or managerial occupations and who are fairly well educated; it includes a large proportion of Jews. The size of their families is not substantially different from that of most men in that age cohort, and more than two-thirds of their wives work outside the home. While the degree to which they share housework varies considerably, most men in the sample are clustered in the 40-49 percent area; these are not men who have taken over housework on a temporary basis, since more than three-fourths of them have been doing housework for more than four years.

CONCLUSION

Considerable changes in sex roles in the United States have taken place since the days when Parsons and Sirjamaki made their descriptions of the typical sexual division of labor. Observers from polemicists to journalists to sociologists have described this change, but almost exclusively as regards its implications for women. That women are increasingly taking over instrumental functions, with all the difficulty, or sense of liberation, or both, that this involves, has been endlessly discussed in popular and scholarly media. Almost entirely neglected, however, has been the meaning of this social transformation for men. The evidence we have looked at in this chapter indicates that men are increasingly being expected to take over expressive functions, in addition to handling their instrumental ones. That men are little prepared for this in their upbringing and in popular images of men hardly needs stating. One of the central purposes of this study is to begin to fill in that vast void in our knowledge of what changing sex roles in American society and in the American family means for men.

More surprising than the changes in sex roles, perhaps, is the extent to which men today share in many aspects of housework in American families. It is worth repeating that these tasks, such as shopping, cooking, cleaning, and child care, are added onto the already substantial volume of housework that men do. The totally sex-segregated family is extremely rare, if indeed it exists at all in the American family today, and there is a wide range of degrees of sharing from one household to the next and from one group of household tasks to the next. Overall, there is extensive sharing in America today, although there appears to be a persistent tendency toward instrumental tasks for husbands and expressive tasks for wives, all other things being equal.

But all other things are never equal. The next chapter is concerned with an examination of how these other things vary: what factors lead men to do more or less housework.

2 Why Do Men Do Housework?

Why do men do housework? As was pointed out in the Introduction, much of the abundant housework done by American husbands is not called that, because it comprises tasks not conventionally done by women. What leads men to take over tasks ordinarily performed by their wives? Other studies have shown that certain factors are important in leading men to take over part of their wives' housework in addition to the jobs they already do, such as changing oil filters, cutting the grass, and repairing machinery. These studies lead us to look at the more detailed results yielded by the househusbands survey. The survey results can be used to test expectations about factors that lead men to do more housework, as suggested by material published in other studies. For this, aggregate results of the survey can test whether hypotheses indicated by other studies are confirmed or disconfirmed by the sample. But the survey results can be used in another way. We can look at the words of the respondents themselves when they were asked why they took over household tasks. In this chapter, then, we will first look at other studies; next, we will compare their results with those of the househusbands survey; and, finally, we will look at the human reality underlying the statistics: the testimony of the househusbands themselves.

FACTORS THAT LEAD MEN TO DO HOUSEWORK

The variation in housework performance indicated in the studies discussed in Chapter 1 suggests that there may be some underlying factors that cause some husbands to avoid housework and others to become househusbands. Several studies already done, some of which are explicitly interested in men's performance of housework, reveal what some of these factors might be: social class, age, a working wife, and parental influence, particularly that of a father. For each of these factors, let us compare the results of various research with the results of our survey.

18

Class, Occupation, and Income Differences

A conventional image of blue-collar men is that they regard housework as woman's work that is beneath contempt. Komarovsky's classic study, *Blue Collar Marriage* (1967), contradicts this misconception. One of the findings of this rich and engrossing report is that in working-class families there is considerable variety in the extent to which husbands participate in household tasks. Over 80 percent of the husbands never or hardly ever share in cooking or doing the laundry; 75 percent never or hardly ever participate in cleaning, and 63 percent never or hardly ever do the dishes. But when it comes to doing grocery shopping or taking care of infants, there is much more variation: 46 percent never or hardly ever shop for groceries, but 36 percent do so regularly. Thirty-one percent never or hardly ever take care of infants, but 36 percent do so occasionally and 36 percent do so frequently or regularly (Komarovsky, 1967: 50). Although there are activities in which very few blue-collar men participate, such as cooking and laundry, there is considerable sharing of responsibility when it comes to grocery shopping and infant care.

Komarovsky cites two cases to illustrate the variety of husbands' housework in blue-collar families. In one family the husband shares a great deal in housework, particularly washing dishes and taking care of the children. In another family, the husband does nothing except take care of the children in emergencies. Concerning the way men feel about housework Komarovsky says:

> [T]he majority do not feel that certain household tasks are inherently unmanly.... It is recognized that some men "feel funny" about certain jobs: it may be hanging out the wash in the sight of the neighbors, or making beds or washing out a diaper. Allowances might be made for such sensibilities, but general nothing that clearly needs to be done is viewed as beneath masculine dignity. [Ibid., p. 52.]

This pragmatism is remarkable because it contradicts so completely the Archie Bunker stereotype of blue-collar men that has been so widely broadcast. Komarovsky says that when such men object to doing housework it is not because they regard it as unmanly but because it means that a spouse is not living up to her end of the bargain. If a man works hard all day, it is logical, in his view, that his wife should hold up her end of the bargain by taking care of the house. As Komarovsky says, men doing housework is "a violation of the norm of reciprocity rather than of 'natural' sex roles" (p. 53).

So much for the sexual division of labor in blue-collar families in the United States. What of comparative figures across different income groups? The 1980 study by the advertising agency Cunningham and Walsh, Inc., showed that there was little relation between income group and the amount of housework a husband does. Whether shopping, cooking one or more meals per week, or doing heavy housework, almost the same percentages of men did these jobs, whether their incomes were under $10,000 per year, over $20,000 per year, or in between.

Income groups, however, are only a very poor indicator of social class. Occupation may be more determinative of the extent of housework participation by men. A study from England by Young and Willmott (1973), for instance, relates occupational class and husband's help in the home. The influence of occupational class is evident in the results of this study. Twenty-four percent of semiskilled and unskilled men do not share in household work at all, in the sample interviewed, but this percentage drops to 14 percent for professional and managerial occupations. Eighty percent of clerical workers help their wives with general household tasks, compared to 64 percent of semiskilled and unskilled workers. This is an interesting contrast to the Komarovsky study, in which blue-collar men's participation in housework is shown to be significant, and to the Cunningham and Walsh study, which shows that there is little relation between income level and housework sharing. Part of the explanation for this may be that social classes in England are far more deeply rooted than in the United States. Social mobility between classes there is more difficult, and classes have developed their own subcultures, including dress, diet, language, mode of spending leisure time, and, evidently, sex-role patterns. There is little subjective consciousness of class difference in the United States, and this lack appears to be reflected in the lack of income distinctions in housework sharing by husbands.

Numerous other studies provide indirect information about the sharing of housework by social class, but this evidence is contradictory. Havighurst and Davis (1955) say that there is no difference in the amount of caretaking done by fathers of different classes, but Goode (1956) says that husbands from "lower-class" occupations share housework less than middle-class husbands. On the other hand, Stolz (1960) finds that lower-class boys have a greater tendency to attribute "nontraditional domestic roles" to males than upper-middle-class boys. Much of this variation is due to how social class is defined, whether as income group, occupational class, prestige, or some composite of these factors.

In summary, prior research would lead us to expect that there might be some relation between social class and husbands' participation in housework, but that this would be revealed not so much in different income groups as in different occupational groups. How does this hypothesis compare with the data produced by the househusbands survey? Let us look at the relation between the respondent's occupation and percentage of household tasks done by him, as presented in Table 2.1

Table 2.1 Percentage of Housework Done and Respondent Husband's Occupation: Househusbands Survey

| | Percent of Housework | | |
	29-40	50-Over	Number
Professional, Technical	29	72	(24)
Managerial	39	11	(17)
Clerical	13	6	(6)
Service	11	0	(4)
Skilled	5	0	(2)
Other	3	11	(3)

NOTE: Chi- square $= 13.53$; df $= 5$; p $= .02$

This table shows a strong relation between occupation and the amount of housework done by a respondent. For clarity, two categories were made for the latter factor, "less than half" and "more than half" of the housework. If there were no relation between occupation and housework, there would be about the same proportion of men in each occupational group who did less than half or more than half of the housework. But whereas 29 percent of the group who did less than half of the housework were professional and technical men, 72 percent of the men who did more than half of the housework were in these occupations. If we combine professional and technical with managerial jobs, 64 percent of the men who do less than half of the housework are in these occupations, compared with 84 percent of the men who do more than half. Men in less skilled jobs tend to do less housework: 32 percent of the men who do less than half of the housework are in less skilled jobs (clerical, services, skilled, and other), whereas only 17 percent of the men who do more than half of the housework are in these less skilled jobs.

These results indicate that the more skilled his job, the more housework a respondent was likely to do. This confirms the observations of Young and Willmott (1973) for England. If the Komarovsky study (1967) is considered in the light of this observation, it can reasonably be inferred that the participation of white-collar men in some areas of housework is even higher than that of blue-collar husbands.

Age

The census data reviewed in Chapter 1 indicated a strong relation between age and the existence of full-time househusbands. Most of the latter, it was clear, are over the age of 60. What is the relation between age and part-time househusbanding?

The Cunningham and Walsh study examined the relation between age and participation in housework by considering how many men in different age groups often did major shopping, varying from 25 percent for men under 30 years of age to 45 percent for men over 60. In the next category, cooking one or more meals per week, the relation is the reverse: the older these men get, the less likely they are to share cooking duties. And there is no relation between age and heavy participation in housework. Some tentative explanations of these differences can be suggested. The much greater percentage of men over 60 who "often do major shopping" is probably due to retirement: men who are less likely to be working outside the home are more likely to shop. The inverse relation between age and cooking can possibly, but not definitively, be ascribed to generational differences; the older men may come from families where there was a stricter sexual division of labor than today. Younger men may be more willing to cook for the family, because they come from times when the sexual division of labor had started to erode in their own homes. In sum, however, these figures are very different from the census data; in the former, the relation between full-time househusbanding and age was unmistakable, whereas for equal-time and part-time househusbanding, there appears to be little, if any, relation. This conclusion is confirmed by the househusbands survey, which showed no correlation between age and the amount of housework done (see Chapter 6).

Employment of Wife

Many studies (e.g., Hoffman, 1961; Weil, 1961) have shown that the willingness of husbands to do housework is a factor contributing to their wives' employment, and they have generally also shown that the more men participate in housework the more likely their spouses are to work outside the home and vice versa. The percentage of married women in the workforce has increased from 16.7 percent in 1940 to 45.8 percent in 1976 (U.S. Bureau of the Census, 1976:391)). It is at present more than 50 percent. One would expect an increase in the amount of time spent by married men on family care, and in fact this has happened. The Cunningham and Walsh report studied housework participation of husbands whose wives were employed full time, were employed part time, and were not currently employed. Of the husbands whose wives were employed full time, 35 percent often do major shopping, 34 percent cook one or more meals per week, and 38 percent are involved in "heavy participation" in housework. The proportions of husbands whose wives were employed part time were as follows: 29 percent often do major shopping, 21 percent cook one or more meals per week and 28 percent are in "heavy participation." For the husbands whose wives were not currently employed, 33 percent often do major shopping, 17 percent cook one or more meals per week, and 20 percent are heavy participants (Cunningham & Walsh, Inc., 1980: Appendix, Tables 13, 18, 19). Although there does not appear to be any relation between husbands' participation in shopping and their wives' employment outside the home, there is a very clear relation between the latter variable and the extent to which husbands share cooking and undertake heavy participation in housework: if wives work outside the home, their husbands tend to increase the proportion of housework they do: and if the wives work full time, the husband's participation is even greater than if the wives work part time.

The Benton and Bowles study corroborates the Cunningham and Walsh data. When it comes to "helping to cook a family meal," the task is done by 55 percent of the men whose wives are employed, compared to 42 percent of those whose wives are not employed. For vacuuming the house, 45 percent of husbands of employed wives perform this job, compared to 33 percent of the husbands of nonemployed wives. For "do the laundry" and "clean the bathroom," the percentages are similar: 36 percent compared to 25 percent for the first chore, and 28 percent compared to 20 percent for the second chore (Benton & Bowles, Inc., 1980:3).

Even when wives are employed, though, there is a great variation from one household to another. In one of the best-known studies of the relation between husband's doing housework and women's working outside the home, a great deal of heterogeneity was found in types and degrees of division of labor in different households (Blood and Hamblin, 1958). They found that a wife's working outside the home has the greatest effect on her husband's participation in housework: the median amount of housework done by husbands of working wives, according to Blood and Hamblin, is 25 percent, whereas the median for husbands of housewives is 15 percent. In the words of these researchers, "Husbands of working wives, on the average, do a greater proportion of housework than husbands of housewives" (Blood and Hamblin, 1958:351). But the variation within the two samples must be emphasized as much as the variation between them: it is clear that in many households, husbands do a great deal of the houswork, whether the wife is working outside the home or not.

One of the few studies of husband's participation in housework over time (Presser, 1977) shows that not only do they share in household and child-care tasks when they are first married, if their wives are employed, but this participation, overall, has tended to *increase.* Between 1973 and 1976, the husbands in the sample interviewed increased their participation in six household tasks: cooking, doing the dishes, cleaning the house, feeding children, dressing children, and bathing children. They decreased their participation in only two areas, doing laundry and shopping for food. The increases in three of the areas were quite substantial: 10 percent more husbands were involved in cooking, going from 50 to 60 percent; a similar increase took place in the proportion of husbands who dressed their children, from 72 percent to 82 percent. And 48 percent bathed their children in 1973, compared to 66 percent three years later. Presser says, "There was a net increase over time in the extent to which husbands cooked or did the dishes, but little change in their participation in the other three household tasks. All three child care tasks show an increase in husband's participation, but this is most notable for dressing and bathing the children." (Presser, 1977:7)

Presser also presented strong evidence that supports the conclusions of studies relating men's housework to women's work outside the home. She found that substantially greater percentages of men did household tasks when their wives were employed than when they were not. In all categories of household tasks, the percentages of husbands who participate is higher for those whose wives are "in labor force" than those whose wives are "not in labor force," with the exception of shopping for food. In three of these categories, doing dishes, cleaning house, and laundry, the differences are highly significant statistically. Presser's study, in sum, shows that the pattern discerned by Blood and Hamblin has not only persisted but has become even more pronounced.

The studies cited so far, however, all rely, in one way or another, on percentages to measure how much housework is done by husbands. A more precise picture might emerge from a study that gave the number of hours spent by husbands of employed wives and by these employed wives. Pleck (1979:487) believes that whereas the percentage of housework performed by husbands of working wives has increased, this is not because the amount of housework performed by these husbands has increased, but rather because the total amount of housework done has decreased, as the number of hours spent on housework by the wives has decreased.

Walker and Woods (1976) studied a large sample of households in the Syracuse area; their evidence supports Pleck's contention. Although they used a relatively limited sample, they dealt with number of hours rather than percentage of work done. They concluded:

> Husbands spent an average of 1.6 hours a day on all household work, whether or not wives were employed. Only in employed-wife families with a baby or a toddler as the youngest child did husbands' time average over 2 hours a day. Husbands' time for all household work did not vary consistently by number of children, age of youngest child or employment of wives. [Walker, 1976:36.]

It seems that husbands' time spent on housework does not increase with their spouses' employment; rather, the wife's time decreases. Husbands don't do more; their wives do less. Walker alone (1970) presents data that indicate this. In all families she studied, the average number of hours per day spent on housework by men is 1.6 and that of wives is 7.3.

When a wife does not work outside the home, she spends an average of 8.1 hours per day on housework, and in general her husband spends 1.6 hours. But as her employment outside the home increases, the average number of hours spent on housework by husbands remains at 1.6 percent, whereas the wives' average number of hours drops to 4.8. This diminution in hours spent on housework by working wives is consistent in each of the specific categories tested for. The total average hours spent on housework by couples in which the wife is working full time outside the home is 6.4, of which men do 1.6 hours, or 25 percent. Yet this is no greater in absolute terms than men whose wives are not employed at all.

The picture of male intransigence painted by Pleck is bleak indeed. Walker (1970) has explained the same data in a supplementary, if not more satisfactory, way. She agreed that a husband's time spent on housework does not increase with his wife's employment, but argued that a wife's likelihood of working outside the home increases as home responsibilities decline. When there are no children or children are grown up, women are most likely to work outside the home, whereas when the children are youngest, not only are their husbands most likely to increase the time they spend on housework but at that time it is least likely that women work outside the home.

To recapitulate, two variables are involved for the wives: amount of housework done and working outside the home. According to one interpretation, husbands refuse to increase their housework, and so, when women working must decrease theirs, the total amount of housework done decreases. Another interpretation of the same data is that as the amount of necessary housework decreases, the likelihood of women's undertaking to work outside the home increases. The two explanations are not mutually exclusive. A denial of the validity of one or the other must therefore depend on ideological or theoretical considerations.

A 1977 report shows the same factors at play on the basis of much more comprehensive data. Using a nationwide representative sample, Robinson studied the use of time by Americans. According to this study, between 1965 and 1975 the average number of hours per week spent by married men on family care in the United States increased from 9.0 to 9.7 hours whereas the average number of hours per week spent by married employed women on family care decreased from 28.8 to 24.9 hours. In absolute terms, then, the amount of housework done by husbands of employed wives increased, and it increased in relative terms as well, from 24 percent to 28 percent. These figures corroborate the data yielded by the comprehensive Cunningham and Walsh study. Both are based on large, representative samples, and can be taken as fairly conclusive evidence.

On the basis of studies made to date, then, we should expect that as wives increase the amount of time they work outside the home, their husbands will take over a larger share of the housework. This expectation is borne out by the househusbands survey. In Table 2.2 the percentage of housework performed by the respondent husband is compared with his wife's employment outside the home.

Table 2.2 Percentage of Housework Done by Husband by Employment of Wife: Househusbands Survey

	Percent of Housework		
Wife's Employment Status	20-49	50-Over	Total
Not Employed outside Home	16	2	18
Employed outside Home	22	16	38
Total	38	18	56

NOTE: Chi- square =5.4; df =1; p =less than .05

This table shows that a househusband increases his share of household tasks when his wife is employed outside the home. The same factors appear to be at play in these households as in the households studied by the researchers reviewed earlier. This does not show us, however, what the causal relationship is. We cannot conclude, on the basis of this table, whether the wives are working outside the home because their husbands have agreed to do more housework, or whether the men do more housework because their wives are employed outside the home. In the final section of this chapter, we will look to the words of the respondents themselves for an answer to this question.

Role Models

One of the ways in which people learn how to be male or female is by imitating the behavior of the parent of the same sex. This is a process called identification, and the idea has its roots in the theories of Freud. In its simplest terms, this theory suggests that a child resolves infantile erotic attachment to the parent of the opposite sex by repressing these feelings and by using the parent of the same sex as a kind of model of behavior. Many of the details of the process have been revised by supporters and enemies of Freud, but the end result of the Oedipus or Electra complex is questioned by few: boys take their fathers as models of behavior, boys take their fathers' roles as models for their own. Hence the sociological term "role model": a role model, where sex roles are involved, is a like-sex parent (or other person) whose social behavior is imitated.

For boys, identification with a paternal role model is complicated by several factors. As an infant, a boy's first identification is with his mother, and his identification with his father involves a struggle against this earlier feminine identification. This is why many of the occupations boys dream of occupying in adulthood are compulsively and stereotypically masculine, such as that of fireman, soldier, and policeman. Parsons and Bales (1955) suggest that this need to switch identification from a female figure to a male figure, and the lack of any comparable need for girls, explains the higher rates of psychosexual disorders among males. This is further complicated by the fact that a boy's father is away from home, at work, most of the time. Boys have to develop ideas of masculinity from guidelines offered by women—their mothers, sisters, and female peers—and from images offered by society at large, including "superheroes." Superman and Batman, for example, are fantasy males who take the place of an absent father. David Lynn (1973) sums up this complicated situation in the following words:

> Those boys who do manage to shift from mother to masculine identification discover that they do not belong to the same sex category to which the mother belongs, but rather to the sex category to which the father belongs. The young boy discovers that he is no longer almost completely in a woman's world characterized by the maternal care received during infancy, but is now increasingly in a man's world. The boy is under considerable pressure to adopt the masculine role, to be a "little man." These demands are made on him despite the fact that he has fewer men than women models for identification... Despite the shortage of male models, a somewhat stereotyped and conventional masculine role is nonetheless spelled out for him. [P. 91.]

This theoretical description of the process of boys' sex-role identification has been empirically tested and corroborated (see, e.g., Heilbrun, 1965).

It would be easy to overstate the determining aspects of role modeling. Human beings are not carbon copies of their parents, fortunately, and the influence of a role model is not to make a boy, when he grows up, into a younger version of his father. In other words, people imitate their role models, but not passively. There is a creative, innovative, and interpretive aspect to role modeling, which accounts for much of the variety in human behavior. If sex-role models were the only force determining how men and women acted, sex roles would never change, because each generation would precisely replicate the previous one.

So we should expect that there is a tendency for sex-role models to have an important effect on how men act in a masculine fashion, but that this is not the only factor involved. Other research has borne out this expectation and has indicated other factors that will tend to increase the importance of a father's being a role model on his son's behavior. For instance, Rau (1960) showed that a boy is more likely to identify with his father to the extent that his father is involved in child rearing. Bronfenbrenner (1960) makes a similar point: children are more likely to imitate the behavior of like-sex parents when they receive encouragement for doing so. And Hoffman (1961) concludes that when their relations are affectionate, there is a very strong correlation between the behavior of father and son. The counterpart of this is the conclusion by Rapoport and Rapoport (1976) in their study of dual career families, that

> The only factor that conspicuously differentiated the dual career husbands from their conventional counterparts was the tendency for dual career husbands to have had a particularly warm relationship with their mothers ... ..a pattern of warmth and sympathy seems to have been established that may have laid the foundations for subsequent responsiveness to the aspirations of their wives. [P. 44.]

On the basis of what we know about sex-role modeling, we could expect that a father's performance of household tasks would have an important effect on his son's performance of these tasks when he grows up and marries, but that many other factors intervene to determine the strength of this correlation.

To test the importance of role modeling for the amount of housework done by a househusband, the percentage of housework done by the respondent househusband was compared with the percentage of housework done by his father. As a father's share increases, there is a tendency for a son's share to increase. This tendency amounts to a moderately strong relationship and one that is statistically significant. The correlation coefficient is .25, which is significant at the .03 level. This evidence confirms our expectations about the importance of role modeling for the extent of a man's participation in housework. It is important, but it is far from being the determining factor. A househusbanding father is more likely than not to have a similar son, but many other factors affect the outcome.

The significance of Lynn's description of sex-role identification is underlined by this evidence. If a boy's father has a conventional sex role—working outside the home and absent most of the time—the boy must learn how to be a man from women and from "stereotyped and conventional" cultural occupational images. He must be compulsively masculine to overcome his early identification with his mother, but must also imagine manhood to himself in simple, forceful terms. But suppose that a boy's father is significantly involved in housework, for whatever reason. Not only is his father less absent (particularly if he does extensive child care) but his father also offers him a concrete idea of masculinity rather than the female-defined and fantasy masculinity that most boys must depend upon. In short, a man whose father has been extensively involved in housework is a man whose sexual identity is more authentically based—on role modeling, based on his father—than is possible where women, comic books, and television are the primary sources for sexual identity.

Other Factors

Since the previous research on househusbands is limited, we have dealt in this review with only four factors—suggested by other studies—that may affect the extent to which men do housework: occupation, age, employment of wife, and father's sex-role modeling. The househusbands survey measured other variables that might have a similar effect: a respondent's education, his father's occupation, whether his mother was employed or not, the number of children present in his household, his religion, his ethnic group, and the number of years he had been doing housework.

Only one of these factors affected how much housework a respondent did: the number of years he had been doing housework. There was a moderate but significant relation between these two variables, and it was a negative one: the longer a respondent had been doing housework, the less he was likely to be doing. The correlation coefficient between the two is $-.29$, a moderately strong and significant relationship, but one in which many other factors play an intervening part.

What are we to make of the fact that a respondent's education, his father's occupation, and his mother's employment play little role in influencing the amount of housework he does? At first sight, it is puzzling that his own occupation should play an important part, but that these other factors do not. Education, in the United States, is closely related to occupation, and it might be expected that if the latter is an important factor, the former would also be. If the father's sex-role modeling is important, as we have seen it to be, why is a respondent's father's occupation not important?

The most important factor in many occupations, in the present context, is not so much how much education they require as how much free time they afford. Flexibility of work time is extremely important if a man is to be able to take over household tasks. In clerical and manual—and even most managerial—jobs, a man is locked into a time-consuming and rigid routine, which keeps him away from home for the bulk of every working day. Professionals, on the other hand, are more likely to be able to shape their work schedule around this routine of the household. This theme recurs throughout this book, and plays an important part in the policy recommendations that are suggested in Chapter 5. If American men are to increase their participation in household tasks, one of the measures that must be taken is to make their work schedules more flexible.

Thus far, we have seen that a number of factors tend to increase men's participation in household tasks. A man will be more likely to increase his share of housework if he is a professional, if his wife works outside the home, and if his own father participated in housework. So far, we have looked only at the aggregate figures produced by the survey, for comparison to other research. Although these are instructive, numbers can never take the place of people themselves, and statistics say less than the spoken word. In the next section, we turn to accounts of the househusbands themselves.

WHY MEN DO HOUSEWORK: IN THEIR OWN WORDS

In response to the question, "Why did you take over some or all of these tasks?" which followed the listing of the household tasks and the number of hours spent on each of them by members of the family, men were encouraged to speak at length. One of the most striking general aspects of the answers to this question is how unselfconscious the men were. They might have been expected to give high-flown rationalizations in terms of chic rhetoric, or even self-glorifications about how "unsexist" they were. Instead, there was a remarkable pragmatism, simplicity, and straightforwardness to what they said.

Their responses fell into several general categories. First, and least numerous, were responses from disabled men, who talked of housework exclusively in terms of necessity. Second were those who were not very articulate, who gave relatively uncommunicative and, at times, unenthusiastic responses. In the third set of responses, the men denied that they had "taken over" household tasks; for these men, the situation evolved in a relatively unplanned and unconscious fashion. Fourth, there were men who talked in terms of fairness; for these respondents, their doing housework was the right thing to do, in the light of what they perceived to be their obligations. Finally, there were those men who talked about housework with a sense of pride and mentioned an affinity for it. Let us examine some of these responses.

The disabled respondents are those most clearly performing household tasks out of necessity, rather than some sense of obligation. One said:

> *I was home and there was something for me to do*—(35-year-old disabled dump-truck driver)

> *Since I had my heart attack last year, I'm forced to be home all the time—to keep myself occupied. I do [housework] to keep me out of trouble and to avoid becoming crazy*—(57-year-old disabled man, no outside occupation given)

They are, understandably, the respondents least enthusiastic about their housework, because they are most constrained.

As for the less articulate responses, the most positive of these was expressed by a 53-year-old former warehouse supervisor who is at home by choice:

We changed positions—my wife was bored at home and I was bored on the job.

Less enthusiastic was a 39-year-old high school math teacher, who said

Because my wife is working—just to share the work.

The theme of helping out a spouse was reflected in the following similar responses:

To help out my wife—(41-year-old letter carrier)

To help out my spouse, who also works outside the home—(38-year-old social researcher)

I took over these tasks because they had to be done. Also, it was easy to divide up the houswork between my wife and me—(33-year-old temporarily disabled elementary school teacher)

Certain things need doing. I was around, so I did them; also to help...[my wife]—(58-year-old clerk)

The theme of helping out, combined with the necessity of the situation, is reflected throughout the less articulate responses. They are summed up in the following response, which seems to have a touch of resignation, rather than the enthusiasm of the man quoted above who switched roles with his wife:

My wife began working part-time and it was required that I share some tasks more equally, by doing some of the housework—(36-year-old high school math teacher)

Another group of responses expressed the idea that things just "worked out that way." The respondents were puzzled by the question, because for them it implied that there had been some single moment when housework sharing had begun. The following four responses are examples of this:

It wasn't a decision, in that you do this and I'll do that. It sort of evolved that way. Some of the tasks I do are cut and dry, wash floors, bathroom. My wife collects things, which, for my money, is not worth anything, but

she takes care of keeping them clean. I do things like laundry, which I don't mind doing—(29-year-old fireman)

I didn't take over. They sort of fell into place. There are things that I like doing, I've done in the past and I continue to do. Things I don't like doing, like vacuuming, I don't do—(54-year-old film producer)

It started when I got married (this is my second marriage) last April. My wife was working and I wasn't, so I started to do the housework and that's the way it stayed—(36-year-old novelty salesman)

I began to do more once we had the first baby. Since my wife and I both work (in our own business) and share in our work—it just worked out that we would share household duties—(40-year-old publisher)

"Things worked out that way" is a variant on the theme of necessity expressed by the less articulate men discussed earlier, except that here there is less the notion of helping out their wives than accepting responsibility for a substantial portion of housework. Here is the fullest expression of the acceptance of responsibility, in the words of a 35-year-old social worker.

I'm not sure I really took over the tasks. The balance of who does what has changed over the years depending on who's working at the time. It's alternated over the five years. For example, I wash the dishes because I don't get home until 6:00 and don't have time to prepare the meal. We all get hungry by 6:00, so my wife prepares it. Yet, I have somewhat of a belief in sharing in household tasks, so I pick up from there and usually do more of the work in the evenings with the kids because she's done more during the day—especially over the last couple of years where I've been working full-time and she's been working part-time; she also does more of other things, such as cleaning up. She likes the garden more than I do—it's kind of her garden. I, in the past, have done more cooking since I am home more.

Among those who denied that there had been a particular moment when household tasks were taken over were some men who talked about early experiences in their lives that trained them for doing housework and raised their expectations. Here are two of these responses:

> *I had responsibilities similar to this when I was growing up. My father died when I was about eleven and my mom was working nights and my sisters were just about out of the house so I was pretty much on my own. In one sense, my mother was working late. I would eat over at one of my sister's houses and then I'd come home but I had to take care of the house. I had to do a lot of the shopping, if not all of it. Basically, it came to the position that while my father was sick, I was completely taking care of him. And then after he died, I was doing a little more around the house. So, it just carried over. Some of it may be compulsive reaction but I've just been doing it for so long and I've done it since I got married—*(33-year-old special education teacher)

> *Prior to living with...[my wife], I was almost always in an apartment with another man or other men in which all the housework was shared equally or divided up in some supposedly equal manner. Both of us came into the relationship with that same understanding—that the household work was not presumably done by either person—that we were both responsible for it. It was basically divided up by likes and dislikes and who had time for what. Just an example: ...[my wife] does the vacuuming because I'm allergic to dust and for me, to do it, it would make me sneeze a lot—and I wash dishes because she prefers not to—*(36-year-old telephone company technician)

The first of these men learned the necessities and skills of housework because of a particular situation in his youth, his father's illness and death. In this case, things evolved for him from a very early age, and the pattern in his marriage is simply a continuation of what went before. The second of these respondents had shared housework before in the context of having male roommates during his adult life, so the origins of his experience with housework are in the not-so-distant past. In addition, a note of idealism is sounded when he mentions his agreement with his wife that "the household work was not presumably done by either person." This is stressed much more strongly and clearly in the next set of responses.

Of those who expressed the idea that it was fair to share household tasks with their wives, there were those who were relatively brief in their expression of that idea, those who developed it at length in a fairly explicit explanation of their values in this regard, and those who expressed an ideological motivation in their conception of the fairness of equal division of household tasks.

> *Because I feel running a household is a joint job and when I help do these things we both have time for more enjoyable things—*(38-year-old storekeeper)

> *Out of respect, love and devotion. I feel you only have one life to live, so try and get it right the one chance you have—*(31-year-old wholesaler)

> *To allow my wife to have more time to herself and it is too much for her to handle alone—*(58-year-old contractor)

A 31-year-old municipal budget administrator put it most simply and clearly:

> *I just felt that I should share the work in the house just as much as...[my wife] does.*

A more elaborate expression of the fairness theme can be found in the next set of responses:

> *Because my wife holds down a full-time job and realistically, it wouldn't be fair for her to come home, working 9 to 5, and then have to do all this work. I feel that as long as she is doing a full-time job, she shouldn't have to come home and have to take care of all of the household responsibilities. My schedule is flexible; it's a lot easier to me to do things during the course of the day that she can't do—than it would be if it had to wait until the weekend—*(34-year-old police officer)

> *When my wife started to work, it was a matter of alleviating her [sic] and I felt that I had to share the duties. It wasn't a burden before she started to work but now that she had, I felt that [it] was only fair that I help out—*(53-year-old sportswear salesman)

For both of these men, the theme of fairness is explicitly linked to their wives' responsibilities outside the home. Their share in housework, according to their system of values, is linked to their wives' share in bringing in an income. One can presume that their participation in housework would diminish proportionately if their wives ceased working outside the home.

The next three respondents explain the theme of fairness in more abstract terms. There is an increasing degree of dogmatism, starting with a general expression of fairness in the first and culminating in a declaration of men's "duty" in the third:

> *I didn't take them over, I just assumed them as a normal course in the relationship. There wasn't any special outside event or change in the status of things. I just, having been on my own for quite a while; I just always felt that it was a fairer situation that I would help from the beginning of our marriage—*(34-year-old communications and marketing consultant)

> *The chores in the house should be equal. Just as I go to work, she has work to do also. As far as I'm concerned, the only differences between us are physical differences. As far as chores are concerned, I believe that the woman is stuck to do certain things. We both live here, we both work and I think that we should both share in the responsibilities as far as taking care of the house—*(32-year-old purchasing agent)

> *I believe that a man should share equal responsibilities. In the situation I've been in (this is my third marriage)—in each, there has been a sharing. It's just a matter of how much time each has. I don't see any reason why a man shouldn't be responsible for doing as much as a woman. In fact, it's his duty—*(38-year-old psychotherapist)

The third subgroup among the respondents who cited fairness as their motivation for carrying out household tasks was the set of respondents who cited some form of ideological motivation. This either included explicit reference to feminism or to some key words that have been popularized by feminist writers. An example of the latter is a 33-year-old history professor, who said:

In regards to our daughter, we are very conscious of avoiding stereotyping; that's why we share her care. Although there are things that we do solely: she does the dressing, I do the cooking.

Note that there is no mention of necessity or helping out here at all. The motivation is purely to avoid "stereotyping," which to this respondent apparently means teaching differentiated sex roles. Some men specifically referred to having been indoctrinated by feminists, as the next two passages indicate:

I believe that men should share in the household tasks. I was living with and married to another woman for six years who was an active feminist who got me into this. I have this feeling that housework is not a totally female field. I still can't bring myself to do the ironing or sewing; only if I have to. It also depends on the attitude of the woman. If she is adamant about sharing, then you have to share to preserve the relationship. With the family, it is a necessity to have two incomes except in situations like now when she is pregnant. As soon as we can attain adequate child care, ...[my wife] will return to work. If a woman is contributing half or more than half of the family's income, then it is only right that the man share in the housework and not create two full-time jobs for the woman—(56-year-old office manager)

Because I feel that families have to share as equally as possible duties of the home. I was also trained by two radical feminists who demand[ed] equal sharing several years ago—(40-year-old intermediate school teacher)

The following respondent, a 35-year-old nursery school teacher and college professor, was trained in this ideology by radical political activity and by living in a commune:

I learned to do so for myself before I was married and [I] tended to share household tasks with my wife, largely because of political reasons. We were both in the New Left, supporters of feminism, and it seemed appropriate that I should do my share of the household duties. We also lived in a commune for about four years, in which the household chores were divided by a contract, an agreement by the people in the commune. And with my daughter, I wanted to spend as much time with her as I possibly could and do the same things that my wife was doing.

Perhaps, to emphasize that the categories distinguished above are not entirely clear-cut, it would be worthwhile to cite the following response, which shows a combination of the themes discussed:

Probably for two reasons. One, probably the main reason, is I feel for the equality, the women's lib thing, I was for it even before it came about. The second reason is that I sort of like some of it. You do it and get immediate results. I sort of like it, I wouldn't want to make a living doing it, I get a sort of satisfaction. The only other thing is that I was a bachelor until I was 30; from about 23 doing most of it for myself. I know for some people that would be enough reason to get married, but I have never felt that way. I never felt that one of the reasons for getting married was to get a woman to do all of this work—(40-year-old educational research and materials developer)

This respondent clearly has an ideological motivation, but he also cites the fact that before his marriage he got used to doing the housework, reflecting the theme of "it just worked out that way." In addition, he points out that he enjoys it, and that he derives satisfaction from certain aspects of the work he does at home. The latter idea comes through most clearly in the last group of responses to the question.

A 43-year-old fireman says:

Because I enjoy the cooking. I am also now able to share the workload and responsibilities of housework.

And a 32-year-old high school art teacher develops the idea further:

I enjoy them. When I first got married, I would only, maybe, wash and dry dishes. We've been married for 10 years. As the years went on, I became more interested in cooking, in taking care of the kids. It seems more natural for me. When I was growing up, it was said that women do these things more naturally. I found out that it's not true. And I happen to be good at them.

For others, not only do they enjoy the housework, they express the idea that they can do it better than their spouses. A 31-year-old ship cargo broker says:

I'm the neater of the two of us.... I don't like to see dust-balls rolling in the halls.

And one respondendent expresses a craftsman's pride in the superiority of his performance over his wife's:

Firstly, my time is broader than ... [my wife's]. She commutes to Manhattan. Her hours are from 7 a.m. to 7:30 p.m. and later. She travels for three and a half months out of the year and I, on the other hand, work four and a half blocks away. My hours are basically from 8 to 3. I'm extremely efficient, I can do it a hell of a lot faster than she can, and although we tried sharing more tasks before, it just turned out that I did not have the patience to wait for things to get done. [My wife]... is fully capable of doing all of those tasks—she can and has done them—but she does them at her own pace, which is not my pace. Basically, in the time that she performs four tasks, I will perform ten, bake a banana bread and have four kids occupied in a play setting—(41-year-old junior high school art teacher)

Respondents in the "inarticulate" group seem to express their motivations primarily in terms of helping their wives out. The idea of helping out in emergencies is much more in line with the kinds of ad hoc housework carried out by the men in Komarovsky's study (1967), discussed in Chapter 1. Although the differences are not cut and dried, the idea of helping out with the housework in times of necessity should be distinguished from the idea of taking over household tasks because it is fair. In the former case, the necessity arises first and the housework is taken over, while in the latter, the idea of the justice of sharing housework tends to come before the actual sharing. In a word, the first approach is practical and the second is idealistic.

Rather distinct from these is the idealism expressed in feminist ideology. It will surprise few that feminist ideology is expressed by some men who do a substantial share of the housework in their homes. What is surprising is that of the respondents, only five specifically mentioned the feminist movement or its rhetoric to explain their assumption of household tasks. There may be some who were so motivated but did not say so; but the fact remains that—by their own accounts, at least—few househusbands were impelled to be so because of feminism. More common is the idea of a just division of labor that comes from other, more general, value systems. Most common of all, however, is a straightforward, pragmatic account explaining housework participation. Finally, only one of the respondents mentioned radical political activity, which may surprise those who identify househusbanding with "progressive" or liberal social causes. The overwhelming bulk of the men studied in the survey are not politically motivated, if we are to judge by their own testimony.

The survey respondents cited a range of motivations: necessity because of disability, necessity out of practicality, a sense of fairness, an ideological motivation, even an affinity for the tasks themselves. What appeared was the whole gamut from compulsion to enthusiasm. Although in many cases these distinct motivations are not unmixed, it is evident that the reasons why men take over household tasks as reported by the men themselves, are extremely heterogeneous.

CONCLUSION

Why do men do housework? The number of answers to this question may seem as great as the number of men involved, but some patterns can be discerned. We considered both objective, sociological factors revealed by other research and the reasons cited by househusbands themselves. These two types of explanations should be seen as complementary, rather than contradictory, since few people are conscious of the sociological variables that affect their lives.

There is a clear relation between a man's occupation and the proportion of housework he does. The more professionalized his occupation, the higher the proportion of housework he does. This is necessarily not an effect of education, since the survey showed that there was no relation between househusbanding and education. Underlying the occupational variable is one that has not been adequately studied in this or other research, i.e., the degree of flexibility of time available to a man.

Having a professional or some managerial occupation may bestow a higher income or higher prestige, but the most important benefit it provides in so far as housework is concerned is a greater flexibility of time. Perhaps for the same reason, variables such as a man's father's occupation and his mother's employment status are not important in affecting the extent to which he does housework. A man's class and class background are less important than the flexibility of time provided by his immediate occupational circumstances.

The employment of a wife outside the home is also extremely important. A man does a larger proportion of the housework if his wife has an outside job, and the proportion diminishes if she does not work outside the home. One study (Walker and Woods, 1976) showed that the absolute amount of time husbands spend on housework does not increase when a wife is employed, but another more representative study (Robinson, 1977) showed that the number of hours did increase under these circumstances. Some argue that housewives must decrease the housework they do when they are employed outside the home; others, that they come to be employed outside the home as their home responsibilities decrease. Whichever analysis is accepted, the bulk of published research and the evidence of the sample interviewed, both verbatim quotes and aggregate numbers, strongly indicate that men do more housework when their wives are employed outside the home, following what Komarovsky calls the "norm of reciprocity."

Role modeling is evidently important in determining the extent to which a man will take over household tasks. The evidence of the survey supports expectations that come from other writings on how people learn sex roles. If a father is involved in housework, it is somewhat more likely that his son will be, but this is not the only factor; the outcome would be affected by the variables discussed above and by others as well. The discussion of sex-role models suggested that if boys learn how to be men from fathers who are actively involved in child rearing, they will be learning from a more authentic source than is the case for most boys. It is often said that a man may have to be "surer of his masculinity" in order to be involved in housework; this may be true, but for reasons not ordinarily understood. He may be surer of his masculinity because he has learned his sex role from a man, rather than from second-hand information provided by women and fantasy figures.

The verbatim reports from the househusbands in the survey ranged along a scale from compulsion to conviction. Those least free to do housework were least enthusiastic, whereas those who took over the tasks entirely by choice were eloquent in their pride of craftsmanship. Some men emphasized that their participation in housework came from a sense of fairness rather than an affinity for the work. Those who expressed some ideological commitment to housework were similarly less attracted to the job, performing it out of a sense of political commitment; these men expressed no affection for housework itself, and underlying their testimony was the assumption that housework is something to be avoided. Perhaps most remarkable about the quotations from the men about why they took over household tasks was how few tried to glorify their work with trendy terminology or high-flown language about how "liberated" they were. Overall, there was a straightforwardness and pragmatism that was surprising and refreshing.

By now we understand some of the factors that lead men to do "women's work" in the home. How do they feel about it? Some men see themselves as housework artisans, but there seem to be others whose feelings are less positive. Are most househusbands living a life of frustration and resentment at their new roles, or are they rejoicing in these new-found areas of self-expression? The next chapter looks for an answer to this question.

3 Do Househusbands Like Housework?

Do men like housework? The question is not as simple as it sounds, nor are the answers. The question lumps together activities that are generally regarded as routine and not rewarding in themselves, such as washing floors, with engrossing and often pleasant pastimes such as playing with and feeding infants. As for the answers, on one level a simple "yes" or "no" would suffice, with perhaps an "I don't mind it," as well. But there are deep ambivalences and complexities of feeling about any kind of work, and particularly about one that is so varied and inevitable.

But the question has to be asked, because the increase in men's participation in household tasks demands it. If men do not like housework in general, then they are operating under increasing tension, and the future looks grim for their families. Househusbands would be simmering in resentment against their wives and families if they uniformly detested housework. On the other hand, if men who do housework enjoy it, or at least some aspects of it, then it is possible that doing it is good for them and their families. The answer to the question is important to the future and stability of many American families.

The complexity of the question means that it has to be asked in different ways, and that the answers have to be interpreted in different ways. Three questions were asked in the study to try to deal with this problem. The first was the question, "Do you like housework, in general?" The simplest way to deal with the answers is by adding up the "yes," "no," and "I don't mind" responses. This is convenient, because this type of response can be compared with the results of studies of women and housework to find out if there are differences between the sexes in this regard. But the answers have to be evaluated qualitatively as well, because men often make lengthy qualifying statements that give deeper understanding of their feelings about housework.

Since housework involves such variety, there has to be some attempt to find out what men like the most about it, and what they like the least about it. Two questions asked of the sample are, "What would you say are the best things about housework?" and "What would you say are the worst things about housework?" Unfortunately, it is difficult to compare the responses to these questions with studies of housewives, because they cannot be tabulated in terms of percentages. But a few comparisons can be made.

In this chapter, we will look at some answers to the question, "Do men like housework?"—and the related "best things" and "worst things" questions—and what they mean for men and their families. First, we will take a look at the few sources that refer to men's experiences with housework. Then we will briefly review available information about how women feel about housework, to provide a basis for comparison. Then we can move to the focus of the chapter and examine the responses of the men of the househusbands survey to three different questions.

DO HOUSEHUSBANDS LIKE HOUSEWORK?—WHAT OTHERS HAVE SAID

In the past, there has been very little attention paid to men and housework, as we saw in Chapter 1, so it should not be surprising that not much has been written about how men feel about doing housework. Over the last ten years, however, this limited attention has increased somewhat, both in scholarly articles and in mass media. There are probably fewer misconceptions about the question now than there were in the past.

One of the earliest commentaries on men and housework came out of the feminist movement. In a famous book, *Sisterhood is Powerful*, edited by Robin Morgan, Pat Mainardi wrote an essay, "The Politics of Housework," which has probably been cited more times than it has been read. It is worth looking at what this essay says, because of the formative role it seems to have had in shaping how a whole decade of readers think about men and housework. The gist of Mainardi's statement is as follows:

> Men...recognize the essential fact of housework right from the very beginning. Which is that it stinks.... The more my husband contemplated these chores, the more repulsed he became, and so proceeded to change from

> the normally sweet, considerate Dr. Jekyll into the
> crafty Mr. Hyde who would stop at nothing to avoid the
> horrors of—*housework.* [Mainardi, 1970:448.]

What is the factual basis for this sweeping generalization about
men and housework? It seems that it is no wider than a single
case, Mainardi's own marriage, which, judging from her account,
is one of constant struggle and discord. The message Mainardi
delivers is clear. Men detest housework. They will do anything
they can to avoid doing it. If a woman makes a man do housework, he will be so unhappy that the relationship of the couple
will be stormy and full of tension.

Another version from the same perspective on men and
housework comes from an article by a "male housewife" that appeared in the *Village Voice* around the same time:

> Be you man or woman, a bouncy Home Ec. specialist or
> a disgruntled literary scholar, if you are going to keep a
> nuclear family going in an affluent American suburban
> home, then somebody is going to have to be a traditional
> housewife. And that is a naturally resentment-breeding
> job. [Widmer, 1977:171.]

No matter that Widmer's assertion that a housewife is inevitable
in a suburban home does not square with the facts. The essence
of his argument is that housework is a job that "naturally"
breeds resentment. Does this argument have any substance?
The basis for Widmer's assertions is no wider than Mainardi's,
being restricted to his own experience. He paints a conveniently
stereotypical portrait of a surly male chafing under the yoke of
housework. Although it is not surprising that this article, too,
has been reprinted in readers—it matches the polemical points
being made by the editors of the book in which it appears—it
should not be confused with reality.

From the figures presented in Chapter 1, it is clear that Mainardi is mistaken about men's systematic refusal to do housework. If she had taken the trouble to look at these studies—many of which were in print when her article was published—she
would have been put in touch with the complexities of reality.
This would not have gone well with her polemic, and so she
avoided doing so. But how about men's reactions to housework?
We should expect from Mainardi's and Widmer's accounts that
our respondents would regard housework with such distaste
that their doing it undermines the serenity of their relationships

and the cohesion of their families.

Rapoport and Rapoport have done two studies of dual career families, in the course of which they report that the degree to which husbands of wives with careers do housework varies considerably. As for the problems these men encounter in doing housework, they say that the difficulties go both ways. Here is their observation from the second of their studies: "Men find it difficult to take over tasks culturally defined as 'feminine,' and women find it difficult to allow them to—particularly if it involves a drop in standards." (Rapoport and Rapoport, 1976:367.) The Rapoports' evidence is more abundant than Mainardi's and Widmer's because it comes from case studies. This type of study usually gives a great deal of information about a small sample. It would be interesting to investigate whether such difficulties appear in a more systematic study.

In *Ourselves and Our Children*, by the Boston Women's Health Book Collective, most attention is paid to women's roles and problems in being parents. However, there is some limited information about men sharing one aspect of housework, the job of being parents. The evidence in this book was not gathered in any scientific way, the book is more interested in persuasion than analysis, and the men quoted are not necessarily typical, but a few of the statements show what some men feel about child care, one of the biggest parts of housework. One message that comes through is that the sharing of being parents reinforces a couple's relationship:

> This sense of sharing strengthens our relationship and transcends our individual troubles with each other many times. It doesn't make us blind to our problems, but somehow there is Ruthie, and her existence reactivates some kind of life in us that's blocked. [Boston Women's Health Book Collective, 1978:141.]

Doing this kind of housework is not a source of tension in a couple's emotional relations, but instead can serve as an antidote to tension. Not, as the statement goes on to say, because the two of them are locked together by a sense of duty but because of their love for her and love for each other.

Harry Keshet, interviewed for the book, comments further about the emotional consequences of increased sharing in parental tasks for men:

> The positives of parenting for men are that it is a rare

place—probably one of the few places—that men can learn to create in themselves, and experience in themselves how it is to care for another human being who can't give you anything tangible.... It's a humanizing experience that can open up men to more loving.... [Ibid.]

All, of course, is not sweetness and light among the men quoted in this manual, which asserts that "the myth of the non-nurturing male is a real stumbling block for men trying to share parenthood." The discussion in Chapter 2, in fact, does show that there is a relation between how much housework a man's father did and how much he does. The more boys are exposed to performance of housework by fathers and other men who are important to them, the easier it will be for them to do it when they grow up. But beyond the question of how and whether they are prepared for these tasks is the inconvenience housework poses for time which might be spent otherwise. As one of their respondents says:

> One of my favorite things to do at home used to be to sit in my big chair and read a book. When I started taking Gordon and Helene three afternoons a week, I began by sitting in my chair and getting up only if they needed me. But they needed me so often that my afternoons were one long frustration. Now I've given up on "getting things done" on my afternoons with the kids, which makes my time more peaceful, but I wonder when I'll get to read a book again. [Ibid.:143.]

These, then, are some of the ambivalences that should be expected of a systematic study of men who do housework: child care can be a source of enrichment for a couple, but it means less time for other pursuits; it can mean a deeper emotional experience than most men have, but it is one for which many men are not well trained.

In the recent past there have been many brief journalistic comments on how men feel about housework, which are interesting if not systematic. For instance, a 1980 newspaper article reported on two Long Island families in which the housework is divided equally. On the one hand, the women in the couples had a great deal of difficulty in ceding power over household affairs, particularly in the kitchen. On the other hand, one of the men reflected that the effect of his doing housework was to improve his relationship with his wife and the morale of his family, and that in addition it was an experience in which he has discovered a great deal. In his words:

> We discovered what we do best. Vacuuming is a wonderful mindless escape, with the jazz turned up loud, but I have to be alone. I feel the same way when I'm cooking. I go faster when I am alone and somehow it certifies that the work is mine. [Behrens, 1980.]

This man's additional points are that one aspect of housework is pleasant because it represents such a change of pace from his job as a public-relations man. What comes through more strongly, and perhaps more surprisingly, is the notion of craftsmanship, the pride in work well done. In this case, at least, housework is far from being anathema to a man who does half of it. It is a source of intrinsic pleasure, as well as good for family solidarity and harmony of the couple.

Finally, the most amusing and sensitive account of a man's feelings about housework is Mike McGrady's *The Kitchen Sink Papers: My Life As A Househusband.* It is a description of a year in which the author switched roles with his wife. He comments on his feelings in this typical passage:

> The year... had been boring, repetitive, dreary and at times just plain dumb—yet, I had enjoyed it more than any year in recent memory. At least I had been aware of it. In living a life of deadlines, a life where one assignment overlaps another, time vanishes. This year I took walks and noted season changes and enjoyed sunsets. This year I became a real part of the family, maybe for the first time. [McGrady, 1975:177-178.]

McGrady here sums up a lot of the ambivalence already noted, a mixture of negative with positive feelings. The statement that some aspects of housework are boring is not surprising; by McGrady's account the negative feelings men have about housework are not all that different from women's. On the positive side, he says that housework's pace provides a welcome respite from a hectic job, and that in doing housework a man can get closer to the real life of his household than in perhaps any other way.

With all due respect to McGrady, though, there are two major drawbacks to his story. His role reversal lasted only a year. Because he returned to his work as a reporter after it was over, housework for him was not the long-term responsibility it is for housewives and househusbands. The writing is excellent and the insights penetrating, but it is not the story of a person committed to housework. The other problem is a sociological one. McGrady is only one man, and we need a broader base of information in order to answer the question, "Do househusbands like housework?" We must also answer the question, "Compared to whom?" As background, we will review the literature on women and housework.

DO HOUSEWIVES LIKE HOUSEWORK?

As might be expected from the great interest in women's roles aroused by the feminist movement, there is far more detailed information about how women feel about housework than about men's feelings in this regard. What follows is a look at the results of some studies of women's feelings about housework.

There is substantial evidence that a large proportion of American women would prefer to be housewives. A public opinion poll reported in *Public Opinion Magazine* (August-September 1981:31) gave responses to the question, "If you had enough money to live as comfortably as you'd like, would you prefer to work full time, work part time, do volunteer-type work, or work at home caring for the family?" Only 12 percent of all women said that they would work full time, 33 percent said that they would work part time, 14 percent preferred volunteer work, while a full 40 percent stated that they would prefer to work at home caring for their families. And of working women 17 percent said that they would work full time, 41 percent said part time, 13 percent said volunteer-type work, and 28 percent said they would choose to be housewives exclusively. The responses of men were equally interesting. Only 45 percent of all men said they would continue full-time work, 28 percent opted for part-time work, 10 percent mentioned volunteer work, and a surprising 12 percent said they would prefer to be full-time househusbands. For working men, the percentages were not very different: 51 percent said they would choose full-time work; 28 percent, part-time work; 9 percent, volunteer work; and 10 percent, full-time househusbanding.

Some might attempt to explain the desire of many working women to be housewives exclusively by saying that the nature of jobs held by working women makes work outside the home less rewarding for women than it is for working men. Yet the levels of work satisfaction among men and women in the United States are not substantially different overall (ibid.: 29). The evidence of this poll is that a large percentage of women in the United States would, if given the choice, choose household work and family care as their vocation. But a public opinion poll gives a relatively superficial account of how people feel and act, and we must turn to studies of housewives to learn in detail how women feel about housework.

Probably the best-known study of women and housework is Ann Oakley's *The Sociology of Housework*, a small-scale investigation of attitudes of forty British housewives in the London area. Half of the women interviewed were working class and half were middle class, according to Oakley's classification. Six of them were employed outside the home, of whom one was employed full time. One of the many questions asked in Oakley's study was "Do you like housework?" which she follows with a series of probing questions about particular aspects of housework. Of her respondents, 25 percent say that they like housework, 25 percent say that they don't mind it, and 50 percent say that they dislike it. (Oakley, 1974:66.) She extensively interprets the qualifying statements of her respondents. In a finding that is generally consistent with those of other studies of women and housework, a housewife's social class has a significant effect on whether or not she likes housework. Some 30 percent of working-class women said they liked housework, compared to 20 percent of middle-class women. Of working-class women, 40 percent said they did not mind housework, while 10 percent of middle-class respondents said this. And 30 percent of the working-class women said they disliked housework, in contrast to 70 percent of middle-class women who said this. (Oakley, 1974:66.) It is evident that housewives from the middle class are much less apt to like housework than working-class housewives.

Komarovsky's study, which was discussed in Chapter 2, addresses the question whether wives of blue-collar workers like housework. Overall, 20 percent of the wives she interviewed expressed a dislike for housework, somewhat lower than Oakley's 30 percent of working-class wives. Education made a difference in whether or not they disliked housework: 24 percent of the high school graduates in the sample said that they disliked it, compared to 18 percent of those who had not completed high school. (Komarovsky, 1967:56.) The effect of education on women's like or dislike of housework has been noted by many other writers. One of the main reasons for blue-collar wives' general acceptance of housework and the role of housewife, according to Komarovsky, is that among working-class people a job is less often thought of as a measure of social worth. It may be a means to a good life based on a good wage, but it is not looked at as a badge of respect. Consequently, it is less likely for these wives to look to work outside the home as a source of more fulfillment than they can get from the job of housewife. This is particularly true because the status of housewife is one that is respected in the blue-collar community and a source of considerable domestic power. Whatever the reason, Komarovsky's results are similar to those of Oakley, showing the effects of education and social class on women's feelings about housework.

More recently, a large-scale study has shown results that are not consistent with Oakley's, showing instead far more positive opinions about housework. Iglehart (1979) found that in 1976, 50 percent of 337 housewives interviewed said that they liked housework, which was a decrease from 68 percent in 1957. Negative feelings were very low: 5 percent in 1957 and 6 percent in 1976. The attitudes of these housewives, as in the studies by Oakley and Komarovsky, were affected by income and education. For the women interviewed in 1976, the percentage of women with positive attitudes toward housework was 52 percent for low-income women, 50 percent for middle-income women, and 48 percent for high-income women. Of those with less than a high school education, 68 percent had a positive opinion about housework, whereas for women with a high school education the percentage was 47, and for college graduates it dropped to 34 percent. Even though the study shows that housewives like housework less than they used to, it appears that more American women like it than the British housewives interviewed by Oakley. Purely on the basis of numbers, Iglehart's should be used as the basis of comparison, because it reports on interviews with eight times as many people as Oakley.

However, the tabulation of Iglehart's data makes them very hard to compare. Iglehart specified only "cooking, sewing, and keeping the house" and excluded child care. "Positive feelings" about housework include "unqualified or qualified liking (like housework all the time, most of the time, or like certain aspects—no dislike mentioned)." (Iglehart, 1979:4.) In her appendix, Oakley does not make it very clear how she interpreted responses to fall into the three categories of liking, not minding, and disliking. From her text, however, it is clear that she is anxious to find discontent in even the most contented of answers, and it is likely that her criteria for saying that a woman likes housework are much more rigorous than Iglehart's.

Probably the best study of housewives to date is Helen Z. Lopata's *Occupation: Housewife* (1971). It is extraordinarily detailed and sensitive, as well as living up to the highest scientific standards in the rigor of its method and its refreshing freedom from ideological cant. Typically, it would be fruitless to search in it for a simple "yes" or "no" examination of whether or not housewives like housework. Instead, the study looks in great detail at what housewives regard as some of the more satisfying and less satisfying aspects of housework. What these women see as the greatest satisfaction in their role is their involvement with their children, with 38 percent of the responses mentioning some aspect of child rearing. Marriage relations are relatively unimportant as a source of satisfaction for the homemaker, with only 9 percent of the responses referring to it. But 21 percent referred to personal relations in a rather broader context, including love, response of others, appreciation, being needed, and the ability to satisfy and make a happy family. (Lopata, 1971:205.)

This brief summary of studies of how housewives feel about housework provides a basis for hypotheses regarding how men are likely to feel about housework. First, if men's feelings are similar to women's, there should be a good deal of variation, with some men saying that they like housework and others saying that they do not, with a certain percentage saying they do not mind it. The ratios should be 25 percent "like," 25 percent "don't mind," and 50 percent "dislike," if we use Oakley's research as a basis for our hypothesis. Second, we should expect variety in men's likes and dislikes, with some aspects, such as child care, being regarded as more fulfilling than others. With these hypotheses in mind, we can look at the responses of men in the sample of househusbands.

It is important to make hypotheses, because if they are disproven, the conclusion that housework is fundamentally different for men is inescapable. On the other hand, if the hypothetical patterns of answers do emerge among househusbands, then it would seem that men's feelings about housework are not all that different from the feelings of housewives. This conclusion would be important for two reasons. First, it would mean that sex-role training, the identification discussed in Chapter 2, does not extend to feelings about housework, and thus is more flexible than is commonly assumed. Also, it would mean that househusbands are not operating under conditions of greater strain than women in a similar position, meaning that they are not a disruptive force in the family.

DO HOUSEHUSBANDS LIKE HOUSEWORK? — SURVEY RESULTS

The initial responses to the question about whether or not the respondent likes housework tend to be "yes," "no," or "I don't mind it," but there are often extensive additional comments. The answers can therefore be both tabulated, for comparison with other results, and discussed in terms of the content of the extensive answers.

If men are as hostile to housework in all of its manifestations as some have asserted, we should expect that men who do housework will regard it with displeasure. Of the sample interviewed, 18 (32 percent) said that they like housework, 24 (43 percent) say that they do not, and 14 (24 percent) say that they do not mind it. The first myth that these results dispose of is that men detest housework. For these respondents, at least, there are somewhat more who say that they like housework than the sample of housewives studied by Oakley: 32 percent compared to 25 percent. Of Oakley's respondents, 25 percent say that they do not mind it, compared to the sample's 21 percent. The largest proportion, about half, of Oakley's respondents say that they do not like housework, and this is about the same as the survey respondents. The proportion of respondents who like it is lower than Iglehart's and the proportion who dislike it is higher than that in the Komarovsky study. The latter should perhaps not be used as a basis for comparison, because it refers only to a particular social class. In the interests of rigor, men are only considered as liking housework when they say they do. Those who say they only like some aspects of it (which is Iglehart's procedure) are not included. So we are left with a comparison between the results of the survey and of Oakley's research, and the proportions are roughly the same. Men's feelings about housework are not all that different from those of women.

The qualifying statements about feelings concerning housework are often quite instructive. Aldous, in one of the rare scholarly treatments of the roles of men in society, echoes Komarovsky (1970) in speculating that innovations in sex-appropriate behavior may be undertaken by men with unusual character traits:

> It has been suggested that... it is not the defeated individual but a person with a fairly high self-esteem, flexibility and some sense of controlling his own destiny who would be more likely to engage in behavioral improvisation or "role making." [Aldous, 1974:245.]

The men who make new definitions of how men act, according to this suggestion, are not likely to be followers but leaders. As such, we should not expect them to be parrots of trendy terms, but practical adapters. Pragmatism was shown in the answers discussed in Chapter 2, and the same characteristic is reflected in the explanations of how men felt about housework.

Perhaps the least interesting are those who simply say that they either like it or dislike it. When they are eloquent about their like or dislike of it, they can be touching and humorous. A 41-year-old junior high school art teacher is very articulate about his dislike:

> I despise it. I do not like housework. I enjoy cooking; quick vacuuming can be fun; some dusting and polishing is therapeutic. I enjoy a clean house but the monotony of the routine is sheer drudgery—you keep doing the same things, it's never ending. Women who do this continuously (or men who are home) must go batty. I think some sort of outside experience is necessary.

And a 52-year-old sportswear salesman says:

> Not particularly. It has to be done. It's a matter of doing the job. It's nothing to love or like. It's just that the dirt is there and it's a matter of cleaning it up. It's nothing to

look forward to.

This theme of repetitiousness is familiar to anyone who does housework, as well as to those studying people who do it. A woman quoted by Oakley expands on the theme:

> I suppose you've got days when you feel you get up and you've got to do the same old things—you get bored, you're stuck in the same old routine. [Oakley, 1974:65.]

Another respondent, a 56-year-old cabdriver, finds it very difficult to adjust to being disabled, and has very recently been forced to give up work outside the home. His comments indicating dislike of housework show that he is still nostalgic for his job and still considers it to be real work, as opposed to housework:

> *I think housework is a bore. I like work, but housework? No, no way.*

A 32-year-old special education teacher, on the other hand, is not laconic about liking housework, and expresses himself this way:

> *It's crazy, but I do. I feel like I do it really well, so I like it.*

The respondent is clearly aware of the conventional image of housework as drudgery, and is embarrassed enough at his enjoyment to preface his declaration by saying that it is crazy. A 31-year-old purchasing agent has difficulty admitting that he enjoys it because of the popular stereotype regarding men's dislike of housework, and it takes him a while to state his liking:

> *Generally, it's very difficult for a guy to admit that he does, but to be honest with you, yeah, I would say so.*

The first man clearly feels a pride of craftsmanship that gives him a feeling of accomplishment. "I like cooking. I see it as an art," says a 34-year-old college professor, echoing the craftsmanship theme. And a 54-year-old film producer and writer says that he likes it, but because he only does the jobs he likes:

> *Yes. It's a relief from what I do at my job, the stress of it, mindless activity. I find waxing floors relaxing and to dust. Being a writer, I find the repetitive activities somehow clear my mind from my work. As a matter of fact, when I hit a mental block, I'll defrost the refrigerator or clean the bathroom and then find that I can think. But, I*

add, I don't do things that I don't like.

The ambivalent feelings are also interesting. Here, for example, is the statement of a 42-year-old fire fighter who concludes that he likes housework, but comes to the conclusion by a roundabout route:

There are certain things that I do like and things that I don't, but what I do helps me to enjoy housework.

Another roundabout conclusion is offered by a 36-year-old telephone company technician:

Well, I like to putter, I like to have non-thinking things to do. So, I really don't mind unless I'm falling off my feet, having to wash the dishes, having to do the laundry. See, I don't consider child care and all that goes with that as part of the same thing at all. Yeah, I would say that I like most of what I do. I wish that my house were cleaner and that somebody would do more. I'm glad that it's not me — and I have no desire to put pressure on [my wife], so we just tolerate what we have to live with.

Perhaps it is not a coincidence that the most articulate expression of ambivalence was provided by a 38-year-old psychotherapist. In his words:

It depends on time, really. There are certain periods when I am compelled to do it, because I want the house to be clean. I am not compulsive, by any means. There is something about working on something and getting it clean. There is creativity and a feeling of accomplishment, like in cooking, something I have never done before. I like the fact that I am able to put healthy food into my body. It's really important to spend time with the kids. I see this when I compare how much my father spent with us (8 kids) and how much time I spend with mine. I think it's good to guide them. I think that it's important to share things with my wife, the shitwork as well as the fun things. It makes it easier, it goes faster.

Two other sources of ambivalence are the mixed feelings about housework in general, and the degrees of satisfaction yielded by different household jobs. These are two examples of the latter type:

I hate doing the dishes (because my mother always made me do them). General straightening up is a drag, but preparing and cooking meals can be interesting—(29-year-old special-education teacher at home by choice)

No, because it is work, which I don't like. But there are some aspects that I am able to enjoy—(38-year-old social worker)

Others feel that housework in general has its pros and cons but that there are some redeeming factors beyond the work itself. Here is an example of this type of statement:

I could live without it. I don't mind doing it. I feel I'm showing my spouse I love her by sharing it, and not being chauvinistic or taking her for granted—(31-year-old teacher)

This was the only response to this question that talked of "chauvinism" or any other catchword of feminist ideology. The respondents appear to be generally unconcerned about the larger social or political implications of their doing housework. As a preliminary answer to the question posed in this chapter, we can say that men feel about housework about the same way that women do, with the same proportions saying that they like, dislike, or don't mind it. Their stated reasons for these feelings vary, some liking it for its satisfactions, others disliking it for its routine; still others have mixed feelings, for many different reasons.

THE BEST AND THE WORST OF HOUSEWORK

The question "Do you like housework, in general?" cannot be expected to reveal all the feelings a man will have about it. For a more textured look at these feelings, two additional questions were asked, "What would you say are the best things about housework?" and "What would you say are the worst things about housework?" A considerable range and depth of feeling were revealed by the responses. Let us consider first the responses to the second question, as this is most consistent with the conventional image of housework as unpleasant for men.

First, the terse response of a 33-year-old disabled teacher, who says, "Housework in general." Others were not as comprehensively negative as he. Some men did not say that they dislike housework in its entirety, but rather some particular aspect of it. A 35-year-old disabled truck driver said:

The worst thing about housework is doing the laundry.

A 32-year-old textbook manager said it was cleaning:

I think I least enjoy cleaning. It's impossible to keep the place straight for any length of time. Just the cleaning: I spend more time doing that than I'd like to and it's really never finished.

Dishes were anathema to a 57-year-old taxi driver:

The drudgery...because dishes, you'll always have dirty dishes. You always have to wash them, to dry them; just like everything else...

And one man, a 40-year-old educational researcher, said that child care was the aspect he liked the least:

I am including child care, because it has its difficult and onerous tasks, when they are at the age they are. I think that the worst thing is child care. Housework can be finished, but child care isn't nearly that simple. You can finish that floor or wall. They seem to be getting better as they get older. I can only hope that this trend continues. I found child care to be very much never over, you can't just walk out on them. We're pretty conservative about raising them, don't hand them over to day care centers and such.

But generally, the responses fall into five broad categories. The first is that housework itself is tedious and not rewarding. This is probably the most universal objection to housework by anyone who dislikes some aspects of it. As two of the respondents say:

The dullness and drudgery of doing housework—(41-year-old letter carrier)

It is boring, narrowing, isolating, asocial—(36-year-old college professor)

The drudgery can sometimes be compounded by the fact that others mess up a job just completed. As a 36-year-old fire fighter says:

The kids mess up the house shortly after I have just

finished cleaning it.

And there are times when the repetitiousness of housework makes it seem more powerful than life itself, judging by the words of this 52-year-old sportswear salesman:

> *Having to do it, that's all. Just spending the time on a needless type of occupation in the house because the next day the job is there again. It never goes away. That's what it is: it'll be there after we're all gone. The house will still be dirty with the same story all the time.*

Another theme that emerges is that housework takes up a lot of time:

> *It's tiring and time consuming*—(29-year-old musician)

> *It's time consuming, and not at all creative*—(34-year-old college professor)

The time taken up by housework is particularly irksome for some men because there are other things that they would rather be doing. Sometimes the other things are personal, sometimes they involve other family members:

> *It sometimes gets in the way of things that I'd rather be doing. Maybe just to watch a TV show instead of vacuuming the floor and things like that*—(34-year-old purchasing agent)

> *I find it's a waste of time, in which I could do other things, such as spend time with C., my son*—(38-year-old social worker)

Finally, an objection emerges that is not mentioned in the literature cited but that the author found to be a personal problem with housework. This is the difficulty associated with scheduling housework around the activities of others:

> *Shifting schedule problems*—(56-year-old college professor)

> *Trying to motivate myself to get started is very difficult. It's also hard to schedule things properly*—(29-year-old special education teacher at home by choice)

One respondent says that it is his young daughters who make

the scheduling problems particularly difficult:

> *I dislike those daily miniscule decisions. I prefer more of
> an orderly situation. It takes my girls a long time (and
> many phone calls) to decide what to do. I hate
> that—*(42-year-old retired fire fighter)

In the following responses, the men see the difficulty of
scheduling the jobs compounded by the inevitability of housework and its tendency to pile up:

> *It's a pain in the ass after a while. It really gets to you. A
> lot of the stuff really starts to add up. It's one thing
> before I had the kids. You could do things when you felt
> like it. But now you have to work these things around
> the kids' schedule. If you have to have them, it's harder
> to go shopping with them than leave them home. Some-
> times you feel like there's not enough time to do the
> things you have to do. It's a process of elimination.
> Sometimes certain things have to be left out or I leave
> them go a little longer—*(32-year-old special-education
> teacher)

> *Like everything else, if you don't do things, they pile up.
> So you're forced to do them at times when you're tired
> and you don't feel like it—*(37-year-old contract manag-
> er)

Finally, some men do not see housework itself as having an
aspect they like the least. Instead, the worst part of it was the
fact that it could lead to conflicts with their wives over what
was to be done and when. The 37-year-old contract manager
just quoted went on to say:

> *[Y]ou're forced to do... [housework] at times when
> you're tired or don't feel like it. And that brings about
> arguments when someone is depending on you to get it
> done.*

And this 36-year-old telephone company technician echoed the
message with these words:

> *The worst thing is when it leads to conflicts. Because
> one or the other is not doing what is expected by the
> other. I feel like I should be able to make a reasonable
> criticism of my wife's not doing certain things by know-
> ing that if I do that—it will make her angry, and it's*

frustrating sometimes about who is not doing their share.

In summary, when men are asked what they think are the worst aspects of housework, aside from the few who mention housework itself and some specific tasks, five main messages crop up. These are as follows:

1. Housework is boring and unrewarding.
2. It is always there and must be done over and over again.
3. It takes up a great deal of time that might better be spent on more rewarding pursuits.
4. It is hard to schedule housework with other family members' timetables.
5. It can lead to conflicts with one's spouse.

What is perhaps most surprising is that there is no overt or concealed message from the men interviewed that housework is unpleasant because it is not appropriate to men, that it is women's work. If feelings that housework is not manly are apparently so totally absent, it strongly suggests that in this case the sexual division of labor in the home does not as radically segregate the lives of the sexes as has been thought. Men have the same objections to housework that housewives have, and among these objections the message that it is women's work does not appear.

Even when asked to identify the best things about housework, a few express wholly negative feelings. But most express a gradation of opinions that shade from the somewhat negative through a sense of accomplishment to an actual pride in responsibility. First, the negative feelings:

If somebody else were doing it! Cooking, I guess—(52-year-old former warehouse supervisor at home by choice)

Getting rid of the dirt that's in the house. There's no self-satisfaction in it, period—(52-year-old sportswear salesman)

I never considered it in terms of good or bad...Well...I did consider it and to me it was all bad—(58-year-old retired senior accountant)

Less strong than these evidently hostile expressions are those saying that the best part of housework is being finished with it:

Getting finished! Improving each time you do it. Seeing
how long it stays that way—(30-year-old special education teacher)

The respondent's relief at finishing the job is mixed with feelings of accomplishment at learning a set of skills, but it is jeopar-
dized by family members who mess up the job he has accomplished. These "best things" are reminiscent of the housewives
interviewed by Lopata, who said that getting done was one of
the satisfactions of the homemaker's role. The following statement expresses these feelings of ambivalence most clearly:

The way it looks when you're done. Especially with the
kids because they make such a mess, you know, their
stuff is thrown all over the place. They play with some-
thing for ten minutes and then it goes here and goes
there. And I can't stand that. I'm sick and tired of step-
ping on toys and breaking them. I don't mind a mess,
but it's got to be an orderly mess. If things aren't where
they should be, at least I can find them even though they
aren't in the right place. I like things as neat and orderly
as possible—(32-year-old special education teacher)

As a response to a question asking for the *best* things about
housework, this is eloquent testimony to some strong mixed
feelings, due mainly to the proclivity of other family members
to undo a job just done. This is closely related to the theme of
the inevitability of housework pointed out above. It reveals an
interesting dimension of the negative feelings regarding housework, that much of this is not because of housework itself but
because of the lack of consideration shown by other members
of the family. In other words, it is not so much housework itself
that evokes these feelings of resentment as the behavior of
others.

The relief at finishing housework gradually shades into a feeling of accomplishment, verging on pride. A 41-year-old letter
carrier says, "The results of doing housework," similar to the 15
percent of Lopata's sample who identified "a clean, neat house"
or the fruits of their labor. Sometimes the feeling of accomplishment accompanied the idea that the house is an economic item
in which it is worthwhile to invest work:

Well, the house to us is an asset, and I feel proud of it. It
looks nice and everything is taken care of. And it's pre-

sentable, so I guess it's a good feeling—(31-year-old purchasing agent)

Lopata's respondents, 5 percent of whom mentioned "possessions, home ownership," come to mind.

For a 31-year-old ship cargo broker, gratification comes from having made the house clean himself, in a way that pleases him:

> *Making things clean, puttings things in their place, so that there is some order and a neat appearance. Also, doing housework presents a special opportunity where I can care about doing this menial labor well, instead of resenting these chores that may otherwise seem in the way.*

One of the respondents discussed earlier shows a deep resentment when other family members make a clean household dirty, but the following statement shows that this is not always a source of resentment:

> *Lying on the couch with a tall glass of iced tea and looking over a beautiful, clean house. I also enjoy watching my twin toddlers tear apart and mess up the house as soon as I have finished—*(29-year-old special education teacher at home by choice)

Anyone whose children are toddlers, or who can remember when they were, will realize that this is probably the only realistic attitude to take!

With regard to craftsmanship, a 29-year-old musician feels satisfied at the responsibility housework gives him and states it simply: "The sense of responsibility." If responsibility is the defining characteristic of the househusband, this is one of the clearest declarations in favor of the role of the househusband. The following two men feel pride in the creative aspects of cooking:

> *Being able to prepare meals that I like, since I've been able to take on all the things that have to do with food—shopping, cooking, cleaning dishes—*(38-year-old social worker)

> *I enjoy cooking because it's my favorite task. Being able to share in the responsibilities—*(42-year-old retired fire fighter)

For these men, the sense of responsibility is not a burden but a benefit, particularly when linked to one of the household tasks most commonly described as satisfying—cooking.

An opinion was expressed by several of the respondents that was unexpected, in light of the negative opinions expressed by some that housework's inevitability and pace are oppressive. These are men who say that one of the best things about housework is the *ease* of its pace. Here are two of their statements:

> *You can work at your own pace. You can take a break whenever you want*—(36-year-old fire fighter)

> *There is no time limit. You can take as long as you want to do it. You're not being rushed. You can do a lot of things in your spare time. Certain things have to be done, like the shopping*—(56-year-old disabled cab driver)

One of the sharpest contrasts between housework and the work of most professional men is in its immediacy. Housework is concrete and tangible and provides immediate feedback:

> *It might relate to the frustrating job that I have, but I feel that there's a concrete sense of satisfaction in cleaning the windows, even though I may be worried about when it's going to rain. Even though it's something I've done—something tangible which is much different than the type of satisfaction you get from social work. So, I enjoy the feeling of accomplishment*—(41-year-old social worker)

> *I guess you see a sense of accomplishment when it's done. Especially, when teaching, like at the Board of Education, it takes a long time to see progress. Doing things around the house, with the kids, I have a sense of finality, that I can do things*—(32-year-old high-school teacher)

> *Immediate gratification, of seeing the house clean. The sense of organization—things where they are supposed to be. My brain is chaotic enough without my hands being chaotic*—(36-year-old high-school teacher)

In these statements it is not so much craftsmanship as a connectedness to the work one is doing. There is a familiarity and a recognition that one is giving effort to familiar, loved objects and people. The most comprehensive statement in this vein comes from a 38-year-old psychotherapist:

*The feeling that you've made your house clean. A feeling
that the food you consume is what you've made, created.
And the pleasure of watching your children grow and
not being a stranger to them.*

This set of responses has been saved until last, because it
deserves special attention and comment.

One of the most widely recognized problems of modern
urban civilization is the phenomenon of alienation. In its simplest sense, this means a lack of connection between oneself and
the world around one. Modern man, according to this theory, is
alienated from himself, from his work, from his fellow man, and
from society at large. Part of this is due to the extensive division
of labor, part is due to the impersonality of bureaucracy, and a
great deal is due to the kind of work many men and women do
in the modern industrial world. Seldom do we feel a close connection between ourselves and what we create, and this is particularly true in many white-collar occupations, where work is
carried on in a bureaucratic framework.

Housework, by the testimony of some of the men at least,
offers an antidote to alienation. It is a refuge from specialized
jobs where people make only a small part of a finished product.
In housework, one carries out all phases of work. Work and
home are integrated; one is not working for the abstract value
of wages, but for loved ones. Because most writers about housework in the recent past have been politically predisposed
against it, there has been little recognition of the therapeutic
value of housework. This theme will be developed more fully in
the last chapter, so it is enough to raise it here. The responses
show that for some men, at least, housework is a refuge from a
world of alienated labor.

What can be said in general about responses to this question?
Some men think that housework is so unpleasant that the only
positive thing they say about it is that it is done. Others are
happy when it is finished because of a feeling of accomplishment. Relief and accomplishment are sometimes marred by
relatives who undo a job just finished, but some men have
learned to roll with the punches and accept damage to a spot-
less home done by energetic youngsters. Some men actually
feel pride in the work they do as househusbands. There are
some who seem to look forward to the calm pace of housework
as a relief from the pressures of their jobs. Perhaps most signifi-

cant is that some say there is an intrinsic concreteness, an immediacy in their housework, which is among its best aspects. The answers to this question are like the other responses discussed above: there is considerable range of feeling about housework, and this feeling is as complex as it is ambivalent.

CONCLUSION: YES, NO, AND IT DEPENDS

Mainardi and Widmer would have us believe that housework is so intrinsically unpleasant that men hate all aspects of it, and will avoid it at all costs; if they do it, they seeth with resentment. How close are these anecdotal assertions to the findings of research studies? Rapoport and Rapoport indicate that there are difficulties for husbands and wives in such a role change. The men in *Ourselves and Our Children* are generally enthusiastic about child care, both for its own pleasures and for the way that it integrates them into their families. Similar testimony is found in the journalistic accounts we looked at, particularly with reference to the way in which child care can improve family relations. And Mike McGrady's feelings are mixed about housework, but overall he feels that his stint as a househusband made him a part of the family in a way he had not known before.

Do househusbands like housework? In reference to whom? Polls show that a large percentage of American women aspire to the role of housewife. Several studies measure housewives' attitudes to housework; for comparison purposes, the most useful and straightforward measure was that used by Oakley in her study of a similar sample of housewives. In the househusbands survey, it was found that 32 percent like housework and 43 percent do not, results not dramatically different from Oakley's. The simplest answer to the question is that some do and some don't, and that the proportions are roughly similar for househusbands and housewives.

What aspects of housework do men dislike the most? Its inevitability, its routine, the boredom it engenders, say many. It takes up time that might better be spent on other things or with other people, say others. Others say that members of the family undo work that has been done. Such responses are similar to those of housewives who express themselves about the unpleasant aspects of housework. Rather more unexpected was the assertion that it is hard to schedule jobs that have to be done with other members of the family. Since many of the men in the househusbands survey have jobs outside the home one suspects that this is probably more common with equal-time househusbands than with full-time househusbands. Time is not infinitely elastic, and work outside the home makes it necessary to budget it strictly. This inevitably leads to conflicts.

What aspects of housework do men like the most? The feelings range from a sense of accomplishment and a taste for neatness to a sense of craftsmanship and artistry, as in cooking. The pace of housework is more relaxed, and is a welcome respite from the pressures of jobs outside the home, giving the houseworker time to think. Most interesting are the references to the nonalienating aspects of housework, its immediacy and concreteness.

It looks as if househusbands feel about housework about the same ways that housewives do, in the variety and range of their feelings. This is far different from what we would expect on the basis of Mainardi's and Widmer's essays and the observations of Rapoport and Rapoport. But the results are even more significant than this. Nowhere is there any mention of "women's work", nor of the difficulty of the transition to an unconventional set of tasks. There is a virtual absence of pop ideology about "liberation." What comes through is a series of straightforward, sensitive observations.

These men, with few exceptions, are not stewing with resentment at their household tasks, and this bodes well for their families. Men are increasing the amounts of housework they do in the United States, and if they uniformly regard housework with loathing, their tension will have unpleasant effects on spouses, children, and the cohesion and harmony of their homes. Some men detest housework, and their home lives are probably less pleasant because of this, but the same distaste is expressed by some housewives as well. In general, the results of the study show that the changing roles in the American family will probably not have inordinately bad side effects, and could even be a new source of self-expression and reflection for men locked into jobs that leave them little time for these things.

But men do not react to housework passively, any more than people in general simply react to experiences. Before any conclusions can be drawn about men, housework, and the effects of househusbands on the American family, we must investigate what happens to men as a result of becoming househusbands.

4 How Does Housework Change Men?

Since housework is so commonly considered to be women's work, it is to be expected that househusbands will show some change in how they think of themselves as men. Moreover, one would expect that there should be at least some accompanying changes in how a man feels about his spouse, because doing housework involves not only maintenance of a delicate balance of work but implies unconventional attitudes about what activities are appropriate for women. Finally, for both men and women, housework frequently conflicts with the demands of work outside the home and with feelings about the priority of work outside the home.

In practical terms, the chronological demands of a job are frequently in conflict with the demands of home and children. But there are much deeper potential conflicts, as well. The practical demands of job versus family work raise problems of priorities: which is more important, job or family? This conflict is well-recognized and well-documented for women, whose guilt over neglect of home and children can have a damaging effect on their aspirations for career success. But what of men? It is also well-known that, on the whole, men place a higher priority on work outside the home than on family work. Much of this is because they are socially and legally required to support their families, while their wives have no such constraints. Nonetheless, many may place a low priority on housework primarily because they have never done very much; they may be unfamiliar with its frustrations and rewards. What of men who do housework? Does it change their feelings toward work outside the home, and if so, how?

To explore these issues in the househusbands survey, three questions were asked: "In what ways do you feel different about yourself since you started doing housework?" "In what ways do you feel different about your wife/cohabitant since you started doing housework?" "In what ways have your feelings about working outside the home changed since you started doing housework?" Before we look at the responses to these questions, let us first explore what other researchers have written about men doing household and child care. These sources are very sparse, but they will serve to set a framework of expectations about what the survey will reveal.

HOW DOES HOUSEWORK AFFECT MEN?

Levine (1975) describes a man whose life has been changed by the experience of being a full-time househusband. He left his job as an executive in an insurance firm, and since his experience as a full-time homemaker has become convinced that the kind of career he wants in the future is different. In his words:

> When I quit, they offered me the very best area that they had in the office...Even after I quit they called and made me another offer. I've been back to visit and they say, "Any time you're ready to come back," but I say I don't think I ever will. I know now that I am as good with children as I thought I was, and I'm going to stay in that field one way or another, either with this day care or by starting a nursery school. [p. 130.]

Despite considerable enticements, this man has undergone a deep personality change as a result of his experience with housework, and particularly that aspect that includes child care. Not all men could resist such blandishments, and not all men can be expected to undergo such a change in their lives. But it appears that potentially, at least, the experience of being a full-time or even a part-time househusband can drastically change a man.

The sexual division of labor being what it is, it would be surprising if men were not affected by the experience of doing housework. It involves crossing one of the oldest and most fundamental boundaries in human social history, and we should expect that other studies that have focused on this aspect would have found that men who do housework are changed in some way. However, it would be simplistic to expect such men to adopt feminine characteristics. In spite of many who today tout the virtues of "androgyny"—the manifestation of both feminine and masculine characteristics by both the sexes (see, e.g., Bem, 1976)—the pioneers on the frontier of sex roles are far from androgynous. One of the best-known studies, which looked in passing at men who did housework, found just the opposite. In the words of the authors:

> While the men helped a lot at home, they were not noticeably "feminine" in their character traits. On the contrary, emphasis was given by some to the need for a man to be especially strong so as to be able to tolerate an actively successful wife. [Fogarty, Rapoport, and Rapoport, 1971:371.]

The househusbands survey was not designed to measure masculine or feminine traits, and so we cannot anticipate anything about the respondents' masculinity or femininity. We can expect, in our results, that men will tend to mention the strength they have needed to show in order to adapt to this new and anomalous situation. Not that household chores and child care are in themselves necessarily onerous; it is the need to adapt and be flexible that requires unusual inner resources.

The transgression of the sexual division of labor often has the effect of establishing a more egalitarian relationship between the spouses. This does not mean, however, that they are becoming identical. Calls for "androgyny" and forecasts of "convergence," a social world in which the sexes are indistinguishable (cf., e.g., Benson, 1968), are based on the simplistic notion that the only way for people to be equal is for them to be the same. Identity is in fact equality, but it is by no means the only or necessarily the most desirable means for establishing equality. For the sexes to be equal, as in families where the men are househusbands, they need not be identical in their behaviors, and we ought to expect that specialties remain even where the sexual division of labor has been diminished. This point is made by Fogarty:

> The idea of the marital partners in the dual-career families being dominant in any simplistic sense was inapplicable. The tendency, rather, was for each member to have primary authority in particular spheres of family life, but not along conventional lines of women inside the house and men outside. [Ibid.:371.]

On the basis of these findings, we should expect the survey of househusbands to show men who have been altered in many ways by their experience of housework, but not by becoming feminine or by performing exactly the same tasks as their wives.

In a less ambitious and less well-documented study of men

performing non-sex-typed behavior, Siefert predicted that men would have great difficulty performing child-care tasks. In a study of men who work in child-care centers, he said that men encounter hardship in crossing the line from men's work to women's work. He postulated that this is because there is a contradiction between the status of being male and the status of someone performing child-care tasks. Of a man doing child care in a day-care center, Siefert stated:

> He is a man but he is doing work usually considered feminine...Even though social forces may be undermining these conventions somewhat, preschool child care work remains one of the most feminine occupations in the world. Whether or not the male worker is consciously troubled by sex and stereotypes, he must navigate in a world full of them, and at almost every step he must contradict them. [Siefert, 1974:72.]

If work in child-care centers is supposed to provoke so much conflict in men, we should expect that housework in general and child care in particular would have even more of an effect. At least day-care work is salaried work, whereas housework is unsalaried (though compensated) labor. As such, housework is even more to be seen conventionally as "women's work" than day-care work. In contradiction to the findings of Fogarty and Rapoport and Rapoport, Siefert would lead us to expect that househusbands experience great stress while "navigating in a world full of" sex stereotypes.

Pleck was equally pessimistic about the effects of housework on another aspect of men's lives. He predicted (1977) that while men expand their family roles, there will be tensions unless men redefine and change their orientation toward work outside the home. In his words:

> Expansion of the scope of the male family role without accommodating changes in the male work role will lead to role strain in men similar to the strains now being faced by working wives...Husbands who are committed to equal sharing of household work and child care will find that the demands of their jobs will make this quite difficult...[p. 424.]

Pleck's predictions were not based on any factual findings; rather, they resulted from a particular ideological and theoretical point of view. Not only is such a prediction not based on systematic evidence, it is not even certain that such role strain is

logically predictable. Pleck did not distinguish between the
normative demands of a sex role and the chronological
demands of a job. To put it another way, there is no implicit contradiction between being a man and doing household work; in
Chapter 1 we saw just how widespread men's household work
is. The contradiction lies in the excessive demands on a man's
time imposed by his job. It is one thing to change an entire society's notion of appropriate sex behavior and another, far simpler,
thing to modify work policy to make time more flexible. This
theme will be resumed in the next chapter; for the moment, we
need merely note Pleck's prediction of role strain in order to
compare it to the results of the househusbands study.

HOW DOES HOUSEWORK CHANGE MEN'S FEELINGS...

...About Themselves?

Some of the respondents said that housework had changed
nothing in their feelings about themselves. Here are their brief
responses:

> *I don't feel any changes have taken place in how I feel
> about myself as a person—*(39-year-old social worker)

> *I don't think that I feel differently about myself. It's my
> natural thing to get involved in things that are going on
> around me. No change from before other than the relax-
> ation that housework gives me—*(38-year-old contract
> manager)

> *I have been doing housework since I was a child. I feel
> no different about myself—*(42-year-old letter carrier)

> *I feel no difference in myself, but it takes up my time in
> doing other more constructive things—*(34-year-old
> temporarily disabled elementary-school teacher)

Note that among those who acknowledge no change, there are
some, such as the elementary school teacher, who have negative feelings about housework, where the contract manager
mentions that housework relaxes him.

Because of the way in which the sample was constructed,
there were no men interviewed who were truly newcomers to

housework, and for several, it was hard to respond to the question, because they had been doing housework for so many years:

> *I couldn't say I do. Because I've always done it. When I was growing up the main way I contributed was in yard work. I also kept care of the basement, sweeping and such. Plus I was also a bachelor for many years—* (40-year-old educational research and materials developer)

> *I've been doing this since I was 9. And that started because of a Cub Scout project of family-oriented achievement. My brother and older sister resented me for this. My parents must have seen their opportunity to readily accept and develop such a task force. This is the time when the three of us really got involved in the housework instead of casual labor force prior to that—* (31-year-old ship cargo broker)

But most men did report that doing housework had had some effect on how they felt. Not all responses were directly to the point; one of the drawbacks of open-ended questions, in which respondents are urged to talk, is that many tend to ramble far afield. But even the digressions are instructive. In general, two types of responses appeared to this question, those which reported negative or primarily negative consequences of doing housework, and those reporting a wide range of positive effects. Let us consider the negative responses first.

As might be expected, some of the men said that they reacted to housework in ways that made them feel sad or deprived. Here is the response of a 52-year-old warehouse supervisor at home by choice:

> *The change in the roles has made a definite difference with the kids (some already married—one at home). The looking up to me when I was making a fair salary, I don't have that any more. There's been a complete change in, for instance, "Hey dad, get me a soda," which I never had before. They have no understanding for what we've done. I'm getting a sympathy that I never had before. "My poor dad," they say. "If he was smart, he wouldn't have done what he did, or would have gone back to work."*

It is perhaps worth pointing out that this respondent feels a loss of status, not only because he no longer has what is legally and socially a married man's responsibility and ticket to respectability—a paying job—but because his children sense this loss of respect and apparently let him know it in no uncertain terms. The negative feelings, at least in part, come from the reactions of others, rather than directly from housework.

One respondent reported that the bloom had faded a bit from the rose of housework:

> *I used to really, really look forward to it. Now I do it, I like it, but there's the old shit, like I've got to do this and that. I'm a little more lax about certain things, not as perfunctory [sic] as I used to be. I let things slide a little bit more. I get around to them at a later time. I don't know if I'm mellowing out or if it's finally catching up to me—*(32-year-old special-education teacher)

What is surprising is that there are not more responses like this, considering that the large majority of the respondents in the sample have been doing housework for more than three years. It might be expected that what at first is fascinating and unexplored territory becomes drudgery after a while. In fact, this was the only response received that indicates an initial enthusiasm followed by a letdown.

If we go by the writings of Siefert and Pleck, we should expect considerable evidence of inner conflicts about the appropriateness of housework for men, and of discomfort in public situations where one is performing functions normally associated with women. And yet in all of the interviews, there were only two responses that made mention of this sort of problem. First, here is the statement of a 36-year-old office manager and full-time student:

> *Well, I've had to deal with what I was brought up to believe was "women's work." Since I was brought up by just my mother, I didn't see it in my home, but I also don't remember seeing other male relatives or friends doing housework, specifically not child care.*
>
> *Not that many women were working. I think that it's helped me to not be like that, especially in the child care, rearing of the children. As a man, you have to struggle to treat, view women, or yourself, as an equal partner in what you've seen only women do, as you were growing up. When my daughter was young, I*

stayed at home for six months with her. Even then, I felt strange taking her to the park or the Botanical Gardens and being the only father there.

What is surprising is that such evidence of contradictions between childhood role teaching and adult experience is so rare. Equally rare is the notion that housework is not work appropriate for men, as the sole statement of this sort, from a 31-year-old municipal budget administrator, asserts:

I wish I were a rich man so I can have someone else do it. Very often I feel that it really isn't my place, that I shouldn't have to do housework. Well, my mother did almost everything. My recollection of vacuuming, cleaning was my mother did it. And if it didn't get done, it was because my mother didn't have time...I didn't do it, my brothers didn't. There were rare occasions but the major chores, routine day-to-day work, on top of everything else that she had to do was my mother's realm. And she thought of it as such. Sometimes, when I'm doing housework, I get twinges of, "this is not my place."

This negative reaction to housework is in line with what we ought to expect from the evidence on role modeling discussed in Chapter 2. The respondent's recollection is exclusively of these tasks being performed by women. It should not therefore be surprising that in this single case a respondent feels at times that housework is not appropriate for a male.

There were positive reactions in addition to the negative ones, and in a way these are more interesting, because such a wide range of benefits from housework is reported, and because they are so different. They include an affinity for the intrinsic rewards of housework itself, increased feelings of self-confidence and family solidarity, a feeling that what one is doing is morally right, and a greater insight into the situation of women.

As usual, answers ranged fom the terse to the highly informative. First, some of the former:

I feel more competent—(50-year-old college professor)

I feel better because I can now do things I have never done before—(36-year-old fire fighter)

It makes me feel good to help out my wife. There is a sense of accomplishment— (58-year-old contractor)

A 32-year-old high-school graphic arts teacher said:

I feel more complete, more self-sufficient. I find that sometimes it helps my thinking, by doing something like washing dishes, you have some time and space.

Self-sufficiency for him was described as being "more responsible" by a 36-year-old high-school mathematics teacher:

I've always done it. There's no reason for my wife to do it rather than me. At first, she was home with the children and it was easier for her to do it. I feel more responsible now.

This sentiment was given its fullest expression in the following statement by a 46-year-old college professor:

I've always considered myself independent and self-sufficient. And I greatly prefer sharing the work to depending on someone else to do the work. Also, my wife and I, I believe, feel that we have a real partnership and really help each other and really support each other, and our marriage is stronger because of this.

This statement anticipates the feelings of family solidarity that will be introduced later, but the priority for this respondent is the feeling that doing housework gives him of not being dependent on others. This is in interesting contrast to the frequent complaint of housewives, or those writing on behalf of housewives, that they feel alienated and powerless. What may be true for housewives is clearly not true for these househusbands, and, for the latter, doing housework develops feelings of individual autonomy and self-reliance.

For other men, housework contributed to feelings of being more a part of the family. One of the little-discussed by-products of the conventional division of labor in the modern nuclear family is the exclusion of the male from any but a role of economic supporter and occasional enforcer of obedience. The opportunities available to househusbands for reintegration into the everyday life of the family produce statements like the following, from a 32-year-old purchasing agent:

I feel like I'm part of the family more. Generally, I'm taking on a responsibility of the household which I think should be shared. And I don't think that I'm burdening my wife with the things that have to be done.

The feeling of sharing with one's wife was also expressed by a 52-year-old sportswear salesman:

> *I just feel that I'm sharing, that's all. The family is a matter of taking part, of participating together. It's alleviating some of the burden from the wife. And I felt that if I didn't feel a sense of "de-masculinity" by doing it, it was helping out, contributing. She comes home, she's tired and if I feel that I can do it, why not? Sharing — if you don't share, you don't have a marriage.*

Two men mentioned that it was the intimacy with their children that made them feel good about their participation in housework. Here are the words of a 29-year-old special education teacher at home by choice:

> *I've always done housework, as a child for my mother, and I hated doing it. As a bachelor I enjoyed cooking and did little else. Now I enjoy being home and working around the house, but I wouldn't enjoy it if I didn't have the kids. It is a temporary thing — until the kids are in school — and my own choice — so it makes it much more enjoyable. But I'll do my share of the housework when both of us are working.*

And a 39-year-old high-school social studies teacher put it this way:

> *I feel that I am now a bigger part of my home, in that I do more than cooking. I dust, vacuum, and help with the shopping. And the kids — I like being with the kids.*

Some men reported rewards of a less concrete nature; e.g., that doing housework helped them to gain a greater insight into the situation of women they knew or of women in general in American society:

> *I am in much more intimate and daily contact with the kids. I understand them better, I understand women better* — (36-year-old college professor)

> *I don't think that it's had any dramatic change in the way that I feel about myself. I do realize the amount of effort involved in taking care of children. The house-*

work can be quite a grind. You can appreciate what your mother went through, things that you take for granted—(29-year-old fire fighter)

Two insights concern revelations about the division of labor between the sexes:

I realized what my wife used to have to go through, so I felt better that I could share in the doing of the housework—(42-year-old retired fire fighter)

A man can do housework just as well as a woman can—(35-year-old disabled truck-driver)

In the most abstract set of statements, there were references to feelings of doing what was just. For these men, housework makes them feel good about themselves because they feel that they are doing the right thing. A 38-year-old psychotherapist said:

I've always done it since I was on my own, even when I was growing up. I think that I've become better about it for my partner. It gives me a sense of satisfaction knowing that I am carrying my weight.

And a 32-year-old textbook manager referred to an appropriate "modern male role":

I don't think I've ever felt any different since I've been doing it, since I left my parents' house. Any big change would have come when the kid came along. I guess I really feel good that I do contribute. I think that it's proper, right—a modern male role rather than the traditional sense of mother as homemaker.

Finally, a 31-year-old special education teacher said that he has learned a whole new dimension of daily life by integrating housework with other activities:

I've gained rhythm. I do it to music. You can arrange the work to the way you feel, e.g., mellow—floor, bathroom; good—vacuum, sweeping, etc.

In general, housework leaves some men unchanged, gives some insights about themselves and others, makes some feel a loss of status, and makes some ambivalent. These men clearly feel positive about their more intimate participation in the work of the household. They are particularly happy about

(1) the feelings of solidarity within family and marriage that appear to result; (2) their greater understanding of the situation of housewives; and (3) their feelings of doing what is right. This range of feelings is perhaps to be expected among any group of people who have tried new things in life. What is surprising is how little difficulty is mentioned by these men. The roles of men in American society do not seem to be as inflexible as is commonly thought.

...About Their Spouses?

We should expect that—at the same time as housework affects how men feel about themselves—it will affect how they feel about their partners. On the most superficial level, we should expect this change because the respondents were sharing tasks conventionally defined as feminine. It is logical to expect that performing such jobs will have an effect on what they define as appropriate behavior for males and females in general, and for their spouses in particular. On this level, then, we should expect feelings of understanding, of a general improvement of the relationship through men's insights into women's situation and/or the increase of sharing in the marriage. On another level, however, it would be logical to expect conflicts and ambivalence: ambivalence because of the fact that men are crossing one of the oldest social boundaries in human history, and conflicts because of the difficulty of reconciling schedules. Cooperative housework involves a very difficult balancing of time and priorities, between job and housework and between different items of housework—which are more important and which need to get done more urgently. In short, in an examination of men's accounts of what househusbandry has done for their relationships with their spouses, we should expect answers indicating both beneficial and detrimental effects.

In response to the question, "In what ways has doing housework changed your feelings about your spouse?" we received these responses among others:

> *Housework is harder for a woman than I thought*—(36-year-old dump-trailer driver)

> *I think that I respect her knowledge of what it takes to make a nice house. I think that I respect a lot better what it is to work full time and to take care of a house as well*—(34-year-old communications and marketing consultant)

In this statement is included not only a realization of how much work is required for housework, particularly if it is combined with a job outside the home, but the amount of skill required to do it. In short, the respondent understands more fully the quality of housework, as well as the quantity. The quantity is mentioned in the following quotation as well, from a 57-year-old disabled taxi driver:

> *I feel sorry for her for what she had to do. Now I know why she was always tired—working and doing housework. I could never work and do housework at the same time. That would be exhausting.*

Consistent with the theme of insight into the burdens previously borne by their spouses is that of the greater equality of the relationship. In the following comment from a 40-year-old publisher who is self-employed at home, cooperation in housework is accompanied by cooperation in the home-based business:

> *My wife and I are more equal because we work together in our business. It would be unjust to say that she has to do more than I do, since we do just as much.*

There is a tone of defensiveness to the second sentence, so one may suspect more ambivalence than meets the eye. Nonetheless, the egalitarianism of the situation is referred to in a positive way. Even more positive is the explanation by a 39-year-old high-school social-studies teacher that there are two great benefits that derive from the equality of the arrangement:

> *I feel that we are more like equals. I am happy that we can enjoy two incomes and still get the housework done. My wife has more outside interests, which makes her a more interesting person.*

Not only does the equality produce two incomes, it improves the quality of the relationship by giving the respondent's wife outside interests. A 36-year-old college professor expands on the theme of improvement of the relationship:

> *Very early in our marriage my wife was not working and she did much more of the housework and child care than I did. I think she was very discontented and resentful at that time. When we started sharing housework and child care more, there was less resentment and more appreciation between us.*

In this case, tension was reduced by sharing of housework, because of the resentment felt by the wife when she was doing a larger proportion of the housework. This is perhaps to be expected, because housework has come to be seen as demeaning by some women, and for their husbands to take over part of it shows a willingness to share unpleasant tasks.

At the same time, however, there were respondents who mentioned that their doing housework had led to conflicts. There was no mention of the reluctance of women to relinquish traditional feminine areas to their spouses of the sort that the Rapoports discovered in their study of dual career families (1976). One of the bases for tension was standards, and in the words of a 32-year-old textbook manager his standards of neatness are higher than his wife's:

> *Probably no different except maybe she doesn't keep the place as neat as I do, sometimes it bugs me.*

But more important as a source of conflict was the quarreling over allocation of time, as the following two comments indicate:

> *As long as we have lived together, I've done a large share of the common housework. But it still has been a cause of some tension between us, because we have different standards as to how much time should be spent cleaning house as opposed to other activities.*

> *There wasn't ever a period when we didn't share it, since we've been living together. The one thing I can say is that we argue about who does what and how much time is spent.*

The first, the statement of a 35-year-old nursery-school teacher and college professor, hints that there are different standards of cleanliness in this case, too. The second, by a 36-year-old office manager, suggests that even in households where an equitable division of domestic labor is the goal of both partners, it is not always easy to agree on what should be done and by whom. This, again, comes down to different priorities and work schedules of minimal flexibility.

In our discussion of Komarovsky's study (Chapter 1), one of the insights is that the division of labor in a blue-collar family is based not so much on the notion of innately appropriate jobs as on the notion of a just allocation of work. In the light of this ob-

servation, the response of a 28-year-old fire fighter is particularly interesting:

> *I assumed that if a man does this, it's for some sort of*
> *trade-off; woman works or is going back to school,*
> *which isn't the case here. I guess I'm a little resentful*
> *that I've assumed added responsibility and it hasn't*
> *benefited me. To summarize, I feel that it would be*
> *easier if there was a tangible return on it: wife back to*
> *school or something.*

It is perhaps significant that this respondent is a blue-collar
worker, albeit a highly skilled and well-paid one. He is indicating that he would feel less resentment if there were some sort
of trade-off, some advantage that accrued to him for his taking
over of household tasks. It is clear that his resentment stems
from a feeling that the just balance of labor input has been
upset. He is putting in more than he is getting out.

The final statement—the longest, but also one of the most articulate and ambivalent—was made by a 37-year-old political-
science professor:

> *I don't think that any of these things don't [sic] happen*
> *without a certain amount of conflict—emotional con-*
> *flict. This business about struggling for equality is really*
> *a struggle. You have to combat the dominant image of*
> *your family when growing up, social pressures around*
> *you. But as far as my wife is concerned, it's important*
> *that she work, for her it contributes to her self-esteem,*
> *that she's actually contributing to the maintenance of*
> *the family. She actually earns almost as much as I do. It*
> *gets her out of the house—out into society, which is im-*
> *portant to her and to me. On the other hand, there is*
> *still a lot in me that says, "The woman's place is in the*
> *home." I see my wife as a more active and dynamic*
> *figure in our marriage and in the world at large than I*
> *did before. She's more independent of the family. She*
> *does not define her existence in terms of raising child-*
> *ren, cleaning her house. Her life is partly her children,*
> *partly her house, but largely her occupation. She also is*
> *a much more well-rounded person to her kids. Our kids*
> *will have the image of their father as active around the*
> *house in addition to having a job. Then her kids will also*
> *have the image of her as having a job as well as keeping*
> *pretty active around the house.*

It is not surprising that this respondent voiced such ambivalence over the struggle he and his wife are waging, and that he admits to some feeling that deep inside him there is a hankering for the conventional division of labor. What is surprising is that this was the only respondent who voiced this sentiment; this means either that the others were having an easier time making the change, or were less open about their feelings. The comment "She actually earns almost as much [money] as I do," was made with apparent shock, indicating that transgression of the sexual division of labor in the home, when it accompanies a spouse working outside the home, touches on some very sensitive territory. Required as they are to support their wives and families, many men make a point of pride in showing off their prowess in carrying out this task. When a wife can do it, even "almost as much," it is understandable that this respondent feels uncomfortable.

There is little question that the experience of doing housework affects the relationships of men with their spouses. It is both a source of greater closeness and greater tension: greater closeness because it increases the insight men have into the problems faced by their wives and because some couples feel closer in the more egalitarian relationship; greater tension because of conflicts over priorities and timing; and at least one respondent feels in a state of struggle with himself over the redefinition of roles he and his wife have undertaken. The effects of househusbanding on relationships have been explored; in the next section we look at the effects of the experience on men's feelings about work outside the home.

...About Work Outside the Home?

When people refer to themselves, some of the things they do are more important to them than others for defining who they are. Sociologists refer to this as a person's "primary status," the status whereby they define themselves. Until quite recently, the primary status of American women was their marital and maternity status. As we saw in Chapter 1, many aspects of the female sex role in this country are changing, but men's primary status remains overwhelmingly the same—their occupational status. Men continue to define themselves, at least publicly, in terms of their work outside the home. Housework is by definition work that is done within the home, and it is thus logical to expect that at least some men who are extensively involved in housework would come to view outside work differently. This is not simply a change in their view of their jobs; it is a change in their view of one of the most important aspects of American men's self-definition—their primary status. In order to measure the effects of househusbanding on men's sentiments about what is ordinarily a male's primary status, the survey asked the question, "In what ways has doing housework changed your feelings about work outside the home?"

There was less variety in the responses to this question than in response to questions already discussed, although there was no lack of strong feelings. A few men indicated that the experience of housework was unpleasant enough to make them appreciate work outside the home more than they had before:

> *I think working outside the home is a lot easier*—(59-year-old retired senior accountant)

> *I appreciate my job. I pity anybody who spends the bulk of their time in the home—housewives. I feel that everyone should have a life outside the home*—(29-year-old fire fighter)

The latter statement reflects an increased insight into the situation faced by housewives, an insight that has emerged from numerous previous responses. Finally, a 31-year-old municipal budget supervisor noted an aspect of work outside the home that was attractive for its social implications:

> *I'd rather do my job outside the home. Because no matter how much drudgery I have at the office, there are still people that I give orders to. So, I'm slightly elevated in the pecking order. Here at home, I'm sort of in the trenches. So, I'd much rather be at work than do housework.*

In the studies by Lopata and Oakley, one of the less agreeable characteristics of the role of housewife that emerges is its isolation, the fact that one is working in an essentially solitary occupation. The respondent just quoted indicates that it is preferable to him to be in a social situation in which he is in a position to give orders to other adults. This feeling is a corollary to that of defining oneself in terms of one's occupation. For reasons already discussed, American men frequently think of their identity in terms of their jobs. When this job has a high degree of prestige, a man's self-respect is increased; in this case, his sense of superiority is enhanced by being able to give orders. In most cases housework does not provide such an opportunity.

The strongest message that emerged from the responses to this question, though, was that of a diminished interest in work outside the home, frequently because of an affinity for household work itself or because of an appreciation of being reintegrated into family life. The feeling of being involved with one's children was one of the clearest in these responses, as indicated in the words of a 33-year-old nursery-school teacher:

> *I've been much less interested in being out of the house for long periods of time. I want to be home in the evenings more, with the children.*

And here is the response of a 32-year-old high-school special-education teacher:

> *I feel like I could be happy just working in the home. It used to be thought of as necessary for a man to work outside the home, but I think that I could find enjoyment taking care of the home and the kids.*

While it is still legally necessary for a married man to work outside the home, many couples have made informal arrangements that free men of this burden. As these responses show, such arrangements serve to make men more intimate with their children, something that long work hours generally preclude.

The response of a 35-year-old social worker was as follows:

> *I think I can clearly say that I would prefer to spend less time on my job. If I made more money at my job, I would work half the time and be home more. I guess that's more my model now of what life should be like, of working part time, not full time.*

In Chapter 3 we looked at a study that showed that 10 percent of all working men in this country would prefer to stay at home and do family work and that 28 percent would prefer to work only part-time; this respondent's statement is probably representative of many of these men's feelings. In line with this is the following response, of a 36-year-old college professor:

> *I've always felt that my family was very important to*

*me. I've also enjoyed being a part of the community that
I live in. And participating in the tenants', block associa-
tions, etc. I enjoy my work, but I feel that it's just one of
the things that I do. I've worked at a few different
places. I might change this job that I have now and get
another one, but my family is with me to stay. My
family is more important to me than my job.*

The feeling that his family is more important than his job is
probably increased for this man because of his experience of
being involved with them through housework. It seems that this
respondent does not define himself in terms of his occupation,
and that activities other than his job are more important for his
self-conception. The following response, from a 38-year-old
psychotherapist, says the same thing more precisely:

*I see paid work outside the home less important and less
central to my self-identification than I did before. The
health of my kids and of me is very important to me,
even more so than my paid work.*

Few statements could sum up so succinctly the effect of househusbanding on a man's attitudes toward work and toward his
family.

CONCLUSION

The experience of being extensively involved in housework
leaves few men unchanged, but on the basis of the interviews
conducted, none have undergone the kind of drastic change described by Levine (1975). No evidence was seen of the kind of
reluctance on the part of women to relinquish areas of household work that they regarded as their territory, but no question
was asked to elicit such data. This reluctance may have been
present in these households, then, even though no evidence of
it appeared. There certainly was no indication of men reporting
that they felt more feminine as a result of being househusbands;
whatever else may be true of them, it is apparent that they
have not become androgynous. Also, there were only a few indi-
cations that men had difficulty in crossing a barrier of the
sexual division of labor, in the terms that Siefert (1974) has
mentioned. There was some evidence of "role strain," of discomfort in carrying out two different types of roles, but less than
we would expect from reading Pleck (1977, 1979). Men often

change the priorities they set on family work and job when they are involved more intimately on a day-to-day basis with their families, but this seems to have been accomplished without the wrench that Pleck predicted. In sum, on the basis of the reponses to the survey, it would seem that men are more in charge of their lives than critics of sex roles would have us believe.

Housework changes men's feelings: about themselves, about their spouses, and about work. Some of these changes are negative and some are positive. The negative feelings that emerge are a feeling of a loss of status (not commonly expressed), tension with a spouse over priorities and timing to work to be done, and ambivalence about changing one's role. The positive reactions outnumbered the negative reactions. They included feelings of greater insight into the problems faced by housewives, of greater involvement with children and the household, and of improvement in their marital relationships because of a greater feeling of egalitarianism and sharing. And work outside the home often tends to become less central to a man's self-definition when he is a househusband; he comes to define himself more in terms of his home relationships and non-occupational work, rather than exclusively in terms of his occupation.

In a certain sense, it is to be expected that the positive effects of housework outweigh the negative in a study such as this. After all, only men who do a great deal of housework were interviewed, and most of them have been doing so for five years or more. It would be surprising to find strong and extensive resistance to housework among them, since presumably they will have adjusted after such a long time. This might lead to the suspicion that such a selected sample is not representative, that most men look at housework as anathema. Yet this is not borne out by the public opinion poll evidence we looked at in Chapters 1 and 3. Forty-eight percent of Americans, male and female, consider that a marriage in which both spouses work and both share household tasks is ideal. If there were great latent hostility to housework among men, such figures would probably not appear in survey results.

There seems to be considerable potential acceptance of househusbanding among American men. What are the obstacles to developing the trend? How can we encourage househusbands? This is the question to which we turn in the next chapter.

5 How Can We Encourage Househusbands?

So far, the evidence we have looked at indicates that peoples' values are changing as far as sex-role definitions are concerned, that men are increasingly participating in household work as their wives are increasingly participating in work outside the home, and that househusbanding has many salutary effects—an appreciation of the concreteness of housework and child care, an improvement in marital relationships, and a revised sense of identity that puts less stress on occupation and more on human and family relations. But substantial obstacles to an increase in the number of househusbands remain. Without changes in the some vital areas of public life, we cannot expect that househusbands will become more typical of married American men than the relatively marginal group they represent now. In this chapter, we look at some of the areas where change is occurring and can be accelerated. This chapter is therefore less analytical and factual than those that precede it; in it a political stand is taken, and an argument is made in favor of changes that will encourage the reintegration of American men into their families.

In general, there are three areas where change must and can be brought about: in the area of social values, of law pertaining to the family, and of policies set by private and public authorities that affect men's ability to be househusbands. Value change, the hardest to bring about, will be discussed first, to be followed by a discussion of legal changes, which are relatively easier to effect. Finally, policy changes are the easiest of the three, and the chapter ends hopefully with a discussion of this topic.

CHANGES IN VALUES

If househusbands are to be encouraged, values about what behavior is and is not appropriate for men must be changed. Resistance to greater participation in housework may be almost as strong among women as among men. In spite of a decade of feminist propaganda that housewifery is slavery (which itself is a reaction to past Madison Avenue propaganda that it is full of endless joys), and because of the deep and abiding influence of women's sex-role identification with their mothers, women are reluctant to cede to men a place in the kitchen or nursery. In the words of James Levine:

> It is supposed not only that the home is female territory, but that the male personality is cast in iron, presumably non-functional when it comes to making a sandwich or pot roast, vacuuming a floor or taking care of a child....Kathy Johnson's female colleagues "just can't believe it when I tell them that Bob cooks dinner every night. It's hard to describe their feelings. The only thing comparable is when you go to your mother's house and everything is done for you. That's what they identify with—having someone wait on them, indulge them. Of course, they really wouldn't want it that way with their husbands. They love to talk about it, but they really wouldn't want to change roles. It would threaten their own roles too much." [1975:135.]

It is still a threat to many women to have a man take over aspects of household work, and especially of child care, that traditionally have been performed by women. We know that this resistance is there, but it would require an entirely different study to measure the dimensions of women's resistance to househusbands. The need for such a study is great.

Rapoport and Rapoport perceived this resistance in their second study (1976) of dual career families. They see a resistance on the part of both sexes to men's taking over tasks "culturally defined as 'feminine'"; but they believe that the values involved are much deeper even than this. The devotion—some might call it obsessive and excessive devotion—to work that has been a characteristic of Western civilization since the fifteenth century is one of the great obstacles, as they see it. The heaviest part of this burden has been placed on males, which has deformed men into work machines, virtually deprived of a family life. What Max Weber has called the "iron cage" (1958:181) has particularly tyrannized men, and has replaced the enthusiastic Protestant endeavor to do good works with a joyless addiction to toil. The Rapoports point out that in late capitalist or post-capitalist society, "with the available technology the gross national product can be sustained with much less work per capita," and that values need to change accordingly. As we saw in Chapter 1, there are signs that they are changing; far fewer think that a "real man" must be a "good provider" now than fifteen years ago. But much change is still needed.

Changes in orientation toward work have been noted by many social analysts. In a well-known book about value changes, Charles Reich talked of the "greening of America," predicting the growth of a culture in which "education, work and living are integrated. A man's recreations should be part of his work, and vice-versa..." (1972:414.) Although much of Reich's analysis of contemporary America is superficial and simplistic, he saw the outlines of this deemphasis on work quite clearly, and correctly predicted that it would spread. Daniel Bell (1976), in a much more sophisticated analysis, showed that there is a contradiction between the traditional requirement by capitalism that a man postpone gratification, accumulate wealth, and deny himself the fruits of his toil, and the growing emphasis on self-fulfillment, self-indulgence, and instant pleasure. Opinions vary about whether this increasing focus on self at the cost of work and other public commitments is good or bad, but few doubt that such a value change has taken place. It is a commonplace that many men feel that housework is not their territory, that "a woman's place is in the home." Almost half of Americans, men and women alike, agreed with that statement in 1978, according to a survey reported in *Public Opinion Magazine* (December 1979-January 1980). But it is also clear that more and more men are involved in housework, as the studies by Benton and Bowles Inc. (1980) and Cunningham and Walsh Inc. (1980) showed. Advertising agencies are taking note of this, and there has been a perceptible increase in television and other advertising that depicts men carrying out housework and child-care tasks. We can expect that values regarding this will change even more in the future.

Advertising will probably have a substantial impact on values regarding men and housework, but there is a more pressing need to facilitate this change. An article by Lois Lein (1979) showed that the househusbands she studied lack the social-support networks that they need. Not only are they more isolated from other people than those working outside the home, as housewives tend to be, but they are socially anomalous, and lack the systems of help, advice, support, and counsel that housewives have. A housewife may be physically isolated in her kitchen for much of the day, but she will probably have one or a number of friends to whom she can talk on the telephone even while she is cooking or taking care of a baby. For house-husbands there are no such informal support services, and they are far more socially isolated. Lein suggests that family counse-lors need to be aware of this lack, and to take some steps to counter it. But in the near future, there will be a lack of social networks to make things easier, or at least less isolated, for househusbands. Resistance by men to housework will at least in part continue to be based on an implicit realization of how little support they can expect, both from other men and from women.

Values regarding househusbands, in sum, are already chang-ing. The lack of social support for men doing housework will tend to slow down this change, but advertising depicting men at work in household tasks will probably encourage it. Underlying these factors, however, are a series of changes in the technology of work in Western society that remove the necessity for com-pulsive attitudes toward work on the part of men. Many social analysts have perceived this change, some with alarm and some with pleasure, but to a certain extent the change in attitudes about what is appropriate behavior for men is part of a much wider social transformation that is going on. In postindustrial society, we are freer to concentrate on ourselves and develop personal relationships. It is to be expected that part of this transformation involves men's increasing interest in their home lives and a concomitant lessening of compulsive preoccupation with their jobs.

CHANGES IN THE LAW

In Chapter 1 we looked at figures from the Statistical Abstract of the United States showing that there was an extremely small number of men in the United States who stayed home and did household tasks while their wives worked outside the home. Al-though one of the principal reasons for this is doubtless a belief among many men and women that such behavior is not ap-propriate for men, one of the most powerful reasons is legal. To put it briefly, common law in the United States requires that a man support his wife and children; in general, married women are not required to support themselves, their children, or their husbands. The fact that many women work outside the home does not alter the fact that while it may be economic necessity or a desire for an income or career that leads women to work outside the home, in the case of married men it is all of those factors plus the law. Married women are not required to support their husbands, and indeed are not required by the law to support themselves. Men alone are faced with this burden. In fact, if a man does not work for money, if he stays home and devotes all of his efforts to household work, he can be sued for divorce on the grounds of nonsupport.

The law in New York State, for instance, is very clear on the obligations of a husband. As is stated in *New York Jurisprudence*, in Section 594 on the Domestic Relations Law:

> The duty of a husband to support his wife means, as a rule, that he has the duty to provide her with necessaries. Similarly, as part of the duty of a parent to support his children, he is under the natural obligation to provide them with necessaries.

What constitutes "necessaries" depends on the income of a man. If a man is very wealthy and only provides his wife with the bare minimum, he may be forced to provide her with a standard of living comparable to his own. At the same time, the law expressly exempts women from this requirement. Section 560 of the Domestic Relations Law of *New York Jurisprudence* states:

> Under the common law, a wife has no duty to support her husband, even though his means are inadequate, and she owes no duty to furnish a place of abode for him.

A wife is obligated to support her husband only when he is incapable of supporting himself or is likely to become a "public charge." In short, a wife is only required by the law to work outside the home when her husband is physically or psychologically unable to do so.

This situation is not restricted to the State of New York. It is the case in virtually all of the territory of the United States; the obligation of men to support their wives is the law of the land. As Robinson (1978:5) says:

> The legal equality of the sexes is gradually being recognized in the family support laws. The husband still is responsible for the support of his wife in all of the states, but in approximately one third of them, the wife is re-

quired to support the husband if he is unable to do so himself or is likely to become a public charge.

Unstated and perhaps unrealized in this summary of common law is the irony that in two-thirds of the states, a wife is *not* required to support a husband even when he cannot support himself. The first sentence of the passage is a disclaimer that does not alter the basic fact that men are required to support their wives, whereas wives are not required to support themselves or their husbands.

This is stated at greater length and more specifically in the *Corpus Juris Secundum*, a standard reference work on law in the United States. Under "Duty of Husband," it is indicated that "At common law and under various statutes the husband is bound to support his wife." (Kiser, 1981, vol. 41:404.) In the subsequent explanatory text, it is made clear that this is a moral and legal obligation incumbent upon a husband. A husband, the text goes on, is required to support his wife, even if she has income whereby she could support herself: "The fact that the wife has property or means of her own does not relieve the husband of his duty to furnish her reasonable support according to his ability." (Ibid.: 406.)

The *Corpus Juris Secundum* goes on to say, "No obligation rests on the wife to support the husband, unless a duty is imposed on her by statute. Statutes enlarging the right of married women to contract, and providing that the income from their separate property shall constitute separate property instead of community, do not impose an obligation on the wife; and a general liability for the support of the husband is not imposed by statutes making family expenses chargeable to the wife." (Ibid.: 413.) The first sentence could hardly be clearer: unless the legislature has created such a duty, wives are exempt from an obligation to support their husbands. Even when there is a law stating that her separate income or assets are separate from her husband's, he must still support her from his income, even though she is not obligated to support him out of hers. The inequality of the legal burden could hardly be more stark.

In the light of these legal obligations of husbands in the common law of the land, it is to be expected that few men do not work outside the home. Only the independently wealthy and those retired persons with generous pensions could be full-time househusbands without violating the basic law that applies to husbands and wives. A woman whose husband stayed home and did housework rather than work for a living outside the home would have a strong legal case against him. All married men are aware of their legal obligation, and in light of it, small wonder few dare to flout it.

To state the case squarely, it is against the law to be a house-husband. For a man to give up work outside the home and devote himself exclusively to housework is grounds for divorce. Of course, there are deep-rooted values that are both the cause and consequence of this legal stricture binding all married men. And there are endless rationalizations that make it appear just. But there is little question that there would be far more full-time househusbands if married men were freed from the legal obligation to be breadwinners, or at least if this burden were equally shared in the eyes of the law.

It is possible that the Equal Rights Amendment to the Constitution, if it were ratified, would abolish this form of discrimination against men. But ratification of a new Equal Rights Amendment, now that the old one has been defeated, would not necessarily have such an effect. Even with the Fourteenth Amendment to the Constitution in effect, guaranteeing equal treatment before the law, the requirement that only married men be breadwinners has been and continues to be enforced. It has been argued that even with passage of ERA, women would still be exempted from the draft, and it is conceivable, if not probable, that they would be exempted from the requirement to support their husbands, too. In any case, in the situation as it stands at present—without the Equal Rights Amendment and with the Fourteenth Amendment in effect—the law poses a huge obstacle to the growth of househusbanding.

If we are to encourage men to become more involved in their family lives as equal or part-time househusbands, or to leave the world of outside work entirely and become full-time house-husbands, the law must be changed. Women must be put under the same legal obligation to support themselves, their husbands and their families that men are. It is not clear that the Equal Rights Amendment would establish such a change, and in any case ratification of the ERA does not appear to be probable. Specific legislation to this effect would be required in individual states. The opposition that such a law would arouse, on the part of women as well as men, is easy to foresee. But unless such equal treatment is granted to men, part-time and full-time househusbands will remain relatively few in number.

It seems that American men are caught in a dilemma. On the one hand, there is increasing social acceptance of married women working outside the home, and of men participating in household tasks on a more egalitarian basis. This is both a diffuse social acceptance and one strongly felt by American men themselves. On the other hand, they are still faced with the requirement that they support their wives and children, whereas their wives are not subject to this exigency. Thus, even wives working outside the home are doing so out of their own free will or financial need, to maintain a certain standard of living, while their husbands are working outside the home both for those reasons and because they are legally compelled to. The contradiction between the law and changing values is not a new phenomenon; it has been seen in many areas of social life, where people's practices change more rapidly than the legal system. Sooner or later, the law must be changed to share the burden of family support so that it will be borne equally by wives. Unless and until this happens, there will be relatively few househusbands. Eventually such a change will take place; it is only a question of time, but for the moment, men are caught in a serious contradiction.

CHANGES IN WORK POLICY

In the first section of this chapter, we saw that values are already changing regarding househusbands, and that this change promises to continue. In the second section, however, we saw that there is still a serious obstacle to the growth of men's equal participation in household work—men's unequal requirement under the common law to support their wives and families. Changes in the law do not seem to be immediately forthcoming, but there are interim measures that can be taken to try to encourage househusbands through policy changes. In this section we look at changes in work policy that could substantially aid the reintegration of American men into their families.

In the evidence reviewed in the foregoing chapters, the most serious obstacle to men's household work cited by respondents appears to be that cruel taskmaster, time. One of the greatest sources of conflict between househusbands and their wives was over the allocation of time and the setting of priorities to fit jobs into a limited amount of time. But time itself really is not the problem. It is rather the struggle between work and home for time in men's and women's schedules. With a few exceptions, the schedule of most household tasks is quite flexible, and the real problem is not so much time itself as the inflexibility of the schedules of most jobs.

According to one study, the real obstacle to men's greater participation in family work lies in the rules of the work place, rather than in prevalent mores regarding what is and is not appropriate behavior for men.

> The traditional sex-role bottleneck in the home is one that is more resistant to change than appears superficially. The capacity of men to accept domestic work sharing and of women to tolerate men in these roles depends to some extent on larger social conceptions of male dominance, but it is also affected by other dimensions of experience. Aside from media and diffuse social sanctions experienced, the more prominently mentioned rationale for keeping things as they always have been in the home has been that the workplace is inflexible...[Rapoport and Rapoport, 1976:365.]

In other words, there are relatively few househusbands because there are informal penalties against men who do women's work, and also because the requirements of work outside the home put such constraints on time that men cannot possibly do as much housework as they might or might want to. All this, of course, is in the context of the legal penalties against becoming a full-time househusband. For the Rapoports, the obstacles to men's doing housework may lie more in formal work rules than in social and emotional punishments for violating the sexual division of labor. Most white-collar jobs are of the "9 to 5" variety, in which workers are required to be on the job eight hours a day. If a person spends an hour or so commuting each way, he can be away from the house eleven hours a day. It is nearly impossible to do very much housework in the remaining time. What is particularly ironic about this obstacle to househusbanding is that it is less and less necessary.

In the first place, the construct of an eight-hour day for most white-collar jobs is artificial. It is a schedule borrowed from that of industrial production, in which workers must put a certain amount of time in on the assembly line doing essentially the same thing for seven or eight hours. Most white-collar jobs do not resemble this type of work, and a day in the office can include a few hours of intense work at one's desk, meetings with supervisors and subordinates, and gossiping and staring out the window. Again, although the situation varies from job to job, much of the time spent in white-collar occupations is dead time. It could be used much more fruitfully by being made flexible, allowing employees to use their work time as it is needed, rather than putting themselves at their desks until they are needed.

There are technological trends that will change this wasteful scheduling during the next two decades (see Chapter 6). More and more white-collar jobs are performed with computers, and computers are becoming more and more accessible to the average American home. At the same time, a communications revolution is under way which will make it possible for people to link up their home computers to office computers. In a very short time, large numbers of white-collar workers will be able to do a great deal of their work at home, and will need to come to their offices only one or two days a week, days that they themselves may be able to choose. Within twenty years, a communications and computer revolution promises to greatly reduce the rigid demands on people's time that are now imposed by white-collar occupations. It can be predicted that because of rapid technological change, the demands of time that prevent men's household participation will be greatly reduced. But it is not necessary to wait for decades for the effects of technological change to be felt. There are policy changes that can be made right now.

The National Conference on the Family, which met in Washington in the summer of 1980, issued a series of recommendations for improving the stability and quality of family living in the United States. The most pressing included recommendations aimed at easing the tax burden on certain types of families and at reducing alcohol and drug abuse, but foremost among the policy suggestions was that employers change their work policies to accommodate the needs of the family. These changes include adoption of more flexible work schedules: with paid vacations and unpaid leaves to be negotiated between employers and employees; hiring of two people to work part time at a single job; and acknowledgement by employers of family needs when employee transfers are ordered.

A meeting of executives of some of America's largest corporations was held after the National Conference on the Family results were made public, to try to agree on ways to meet the recommendations. One of the corporation's representatives said:

> We, the business community, appear to be a major cause of some pressures [on families]. Inadvertently, many of our employment policies and practices have created stresses and tensions that have affected the family lives of the people we employ. Sometimes it's as simple a thing as demanding that workers report at a certain hour instead of having time to drive a child to school. Other times it's more complex, as when a company rewards an employee with a major promotion but demands that they uproot their family to another community. [Brozan, 1980:C8.]

It is encouraging to see such sensitivity to the needs of families and willingness to consider policy changes.

Unfortunately, there is a gap between willingness to consider these changes and the action of instituting them. According to a recent report, "Corporations and Two Career Families: Directions for the Future," published by Catalyst, a New York research group, of 1,300 top corporations surveyed, 73 percent favor the adoption of flexible working hours, but only 37 percent actually have them. (Klemesrud, 1981:21.) Nonetheless, these percentages show an awareness that flexible time has an indirect effect on company profits, because it has a direct effect on employee morale. The Work in America Institute published a report in 1980 that reported substantial improvement in employee morale as a result of more flexible work scheduling. According to this report, the Bureau of Labor Statistics now shows that 11.9 percent of the full time nonagricultural work force in the United States is working on a flexible work schedule of one sort or another. These new work schedules involve flexible working hours, "gliding time"—in which the employee comes to work and leaves when he pleases, as long as the work gets done—and several other varieties of variable work schedule. The result is not chaos but improved performance and improved morale. The Work in America Institute found that the "work ethic" has actually been reinforced, because the contradictions between the demands of job, family, education, and leisure have been reduced. Employee morale is increasingly important to a company to the extent that these employees are professionalized; the old authoritarian relationship of tyrannical boss and submissive, resentful worker is more typical of early industrialization than of the contemporary postindustrial age. And with increasing professionalization of the work force, employers need rely less and less on giving orders and more on a worker's sense of professional duty and ethics.

None of these policies, as suggested, implemented, and evaluated, are directly aimed at househusbands. Rather, they all stem from a realization that rigid work schedules are harmful in many ways to the contemporary family. Much of the information on these programs and their impact is sketchy, because they are so recent and because little systematic evaluation has been done. It is clear, though, that one of the major obstacles to easier househusbanding is the requirement of the work schedule, and that this obstacle will be removed to the extent that more flexible work policies are put into effect.

Perhaps just as important as business policies easing the tyranny of time are government policies that make it easier for men to participate in their home lives. Some attempts of this sort have already been made. Sweden has one of the longest-standing and most comprehensive programs to encourage househusbanding and other forms of male participation in family life. In addition to a comprehensive program of day care and parental insurance, Sweden has child-care training classes for boys in secondary schools, a voluntary parental training program in which fathers of newborn babies are given classes in how to care for their infant children, and a law that gives both parents the right to reduce their working day from eight to six hours. Parents may use this time to care for their children, and may return to full-time work when they wish. The parental insurance system is more comprehensive, and allows one parent to stay home for the first seven months and take care of a newborn, while being paid about 90 percent of his or her normal salary. Thus far, about 6,000 fathers per year take advantage of this opportunity. This is about 10 or 12 percent of the eligible fathers. The paternity leave is used more by men in professional occupations and by those whose wives have relatively high incomes than by men in blue-collar occupations. (Melsted, 1979.) This is consistent with the findings of this study: there is more housework participation among professionals than among non-professionals.

Some American corporations have instituted paternity leave options for their employees in the last five years, but few men as yet have taken advantage of them. This should not be seen as a sign of failure of the programs; it is rather a sign of the willingness of employers to accommodate what is evidently a growing demand. As for the slow growth of men's participation in these programs, this should not be reason for despair. There are still obstacles to househusbands in many forms: persistent beliefs among men and women that this conduct is not masculine and that it might harm the men's future careers; the lack of a network of friends and acquaintances such as are available to housewives; and legal obstacles. We are at the beginning of a revolution in American family life, and the first steps of this march are bound to be tentative.

CONCLUSION

Values regarding the appropriateness of men's doing housework are already changing, as are values about the necessity for men to prove their manhood by their devotion to their jobs and the size of their paycheck. These value changes have been under way for some time, certainly since the Second World War, and they promise to continue. In this sense, the future looks relatively bright for househusbands in the long run. A serious short-term obstacle, however, is the unequal legal burden on married men to be responsible for supporting themselves and their wives and their children. It is common for social changes to take place before legal changes. Social behavior is constantly in a state of flux, whereas laws, by their nature, are relatively fixed. Eventually codified laws catch up with new social norms; certainly the law can do little to arrest the change in people's feelings about what activities are right for men and women. But the law can and does serve as a serious short-term obstacle to the prevalence of househusbands in American families. Although it is not clear precisely what laws can be changed and how this should be done, there can be little doubt that househusbanding will be increased if women are put under the same obligations as their husbands to provide support for the family.

Corporations are increasingly sensitive to the needs of families, as families seriously affect the morale of corporate workers. Policy changes with regard to working time and paternity leaves, for instance, have been put into effect, although so far their impact has not been assessed. Relatively few men as yet appear to be taking advantage of some of these programs. This may be attributable in part to their novelty, in part to the potential legal obstacles regarding support that would affect participants, and in part to persistent resistance to househusbanding among men and women. These changes must be put into effect if we are to encourage men to rejoin their families in the United States and other advanced industrial countries.

What of the future? In the next, and last, chapter, the results of the study are pulled together and linked to changes that are taking place on a much broader scale in the world of the family and the world of work.

6 The Future of Househusbands

In this chapter, I would like to summarize the major findings of the househusbands survey and to relate some of these findings to broader social issues. The most important is the place of househusbands in the context of the development of the family, from its preindustrial forms through its present state, and where househusbands are likely to fit in its probable future forms. Household work performed by men has an important relationship to the quality of all work, most notably to work outside the home; some of the insights revealed by this study have implications for the quality of work in the future. The chapter concludes with a discussion of what the future of househusbands is likely to be.

HOUSEHUSBANDS SURVEY: A SUMMARY OF FINDINGS

Before summarizing the results of the survey of househusbands, I would like to anticipate and refute possible criticisms of the method used in the study. It might be said that the men interviewed are highly unusual—my sample is not "representative"—and that the conclusions and observations about these househusbands may have nothing to do with men and housework in general. Sociologists these days have a fascination, if not a fetish, for statistically precise samples with impeccable margins of error, and often mistake their numbers for social reality. My sample does not aim to be representative because little is known about the population; this is no reason not to study househusbands. The primary aim of this book has been to study househusbands, whether househusbands are representative of males in general or not.

Indeed, there is one aspect of househusbandry that is extremely unusual, and it has serious implications for the division of labor between the sexes. Nearly all of the men in this study have work situations that are atypical in that they allow for flexibility in allotting time: most are either retired, temporarily disabled, voluntarily outside the labor force, or professionals who, by the nature of their occupations, can make their own hours. In other words, the only men who *can* be househusbands are those who are outside the ordinary work and time structure imposed on contemporary American males. This heavy burden bears much of the responsibility for there still being relatively few househusbands in our society. My sample is indeed unrepresentative of most American men, but this is due mainly to our being enmeshed in the jagged gears of time and work. Were American men free to make their own hours of work, there would be far more househusbands. My sample, then, is representative of a potential population.

In the househusbands survey, three general sets of questions were asked: Why do men do housework? Do househusbands like housework? How does housework change men? The first question sought explanations both in the words of respondents themselves and in underlying social factors. In general, it was revealed that men will tend to do a larger proportion of the housework if they are in professional occupations: blue-collar workers tend to do a smaller share of the housework. The explanation for this is probably that professionalized occupations provide a flexibility of time that is not available to men in other jobs. Being a professional provides a higher status and sometimes a higher income, but the benefit to househusbands is the flexibility of work time. Men—and professional women who have husbands and children—are in a better position than most to mold their work time to fit the demands of their family time, rather than the other way around. Men who are employed in 9-to-5 jobs are not free to engage in family work even when they want to. In short, professionalism encourages househusbanding. A second major factor that apparently leads men to be extensively involved in household tasks is the extent to which their fathers were so involved, or at least the extent to which respondents *recall* them having been so involved. The implications of this finding go deeper than the rather self-evident observation that a father's behavior influences his son's behavior. In the nuclear family of today, males suffer from the extreme disadvantage of not learning to be men directly from their fathers. Because of the structure of most fathers' work time, boys rarely see their fathers, and the process of identification becomes warped. They learn masculinity from peers; from secondhand sources such as mothers, sisters, and female primary-school teachers; and from fantasy figures such as Superman or Batman. A man whose father has been extensively active in his upbringing is much more likely to have a realistic sense of what it is to be a man. This study did not focus on the effects of househusbanding on children and wives, but such a companion study needs very much to be done. In the light of the survey findings, it is extremely likely that househusbands will raise boys who have a sure and authentic sense of themselves as men. In their own words, the respondents stressed a wide range of motivations, but in various forms, one of the clearest messages that emerged was a sense of fairness. Sometimes this was dressed in ideological garb, but more commonly was stated as a simple sense of fair play. What Komarovsky calls the "norm of reciprocity," which explained the sexual division of labor among the blue-collar families she studied, is evidently in operation here. Men usually become involved in housework because their wives are working outside the home, and they feel that it is only fair that they do their share at home if their wives are helping to earn the family income.

Do househusbands like housework? The main answer to this question was that househusbands are not very different from housewives in their patterns of liking, disliking, and not minding housework. On the one hand, this might not seem surprising, since housework is housework, no matter what one's sex. But there are those who have claimed that housework is so intrinsically unpleasant that men have forced women to do it over the centuries because they do not want to do it themselves. These are unscientific assertions at best, and I hope that this study helps to do away with such groundless generalizing about the sexes. Men's dislikes seem to resemble many of the dislikes regarding housework expressed by housewives. They include the objections that housework can be boring, tedious, and repetitive, and that it can produce problems in scheduling caused by conflicting priorities in outside work, social life, and standards of cleanliness. Most striking, however, were the aspects of housework that househusbands said they liked: the feeling of accomplishment, the affinity for neatness, and a clean home. Particularly interesting were the feelings that housework has a quality that is different from most outside occupations, that it is concrete and immediate, and offers a welcome change from the abstractness and intangibility of many white-collar jobs. In a sense, housework is the opposite of the alienated routine of much work outside the home, which has rigid scheduling, the exchange of work for wages, and a lack of creativity. Housework, in some of its aspects at least, is a kind of vacation from one's paying job, offering concrete pleasures and immediate gratification: a cooked meal, a clean floor, a game with a toddler, clean laundry folded and put away.

How does housework change men? Few generalizations can be made about this, because although few men were unchanged by the experience, their reactions varied widely. Some tension between conventional male behavior and doing housework was reported, what sociologists call "role strain," but it was not greatly emphasized nor did it seem to be a deep and wrenching discomfort; it was more in the nature of a residual ache for some men. But no men reported becoming more feminine or, according to one author's terminology, "androgynous," both masculine and feminine. Probably the greatest single effect of the househusbanding experience was to reduce the importance of work outside the home. For social and legal reasons that have been discussed at length, American men usually define themselves in terms of their occupations; this is one reason why unemployment, disability, and retirement are such shattering experiences for males: they lose the basic reference point whereby they have defined themselves. The effect of occupational self-definition also leads to a relative deemphasis on family roles, so that a man's self-definition is one-sidedly "instrumental," to use Parsons' term. The experience of being involved in household work for years at a time often has the effect of reducing men's emphasis on their jobs outside, and of restoring some balance in their self-conceptions so that their roles in the family are more important. Househusbands seem frequently to have established a balance between home and work, not only in their activities but in their feelings about themselves; they often have more integrated personalities than before. Househusbands often see housework as an antidote to the world of outside work. They react to housework in patterns very similar to housewives. They are motivated by many factors, conscious and unconscious; the former include a sense of fairness and reciprocity, and the latter include the influence of their fathers. But one of the principal factors is time, and to the extent that a man's work is more flexible, he will be more able to engage in family tasks. These are the major findings of the study, and they have far-reaching implications for the development of the family and for trends in the world of work. The findings of the study will be linked to these two areas in the next two sections of this chapter.

HOUSEHUSBANDS IN THE DEVELOPMENT OF THE FAMILY

Of the many areas where the industrial revolution had profound effects, the family felt the impact very deeply indeed. Prior to that immense social transformation, the world of work and the world of the family, were, for most men, not radically distinct. A craftsman or artisan did his work at home, perhaps in a special room or space, but still not physically removed from the company of his family. A peasant went rather farther afield, but his home was on or very close to the land he farmed. Work space and home space frequently overlapped, and for most of the working day the man was not removed from the company of his family.

This was totally changed by the industrial revolution. If industrialism means anything, it means the concentration of machinery and raw materials so that, in combination with masses of labor power, products can be manufactured on a vast scale. Factories are characteristic of industrial production because they are concentrations of capital, primarily in the form of machinery, that can be most efficiently used for mass production. But such a concentration of capital requires that the workers go to where the capital is concentrated. It requires that workers separate their place of work from their place of abode. Work and home become, by necessity, separate. Although in the initial stages of industrialization, women and children formed part of the industrial work force, the most lasting effect of this transformation was upon men. Men were forced to leave their families for long periods of time, to radically segregate work from home chronologically, physically and socially. The industrial revolution removed men from the family.

The growth of househusbands is a sign that this trend is now being reversed. Because of social and technological changes in the world of work, more and more men have increasingly flexible time; their work has not only diminished in quantity, but has changed qualitatively to the extent that it can be shaped to the needs of their families and that family needs are beginning to have a higher priority than they had had since the beginning of the industrial revolution. At the same time as men are increasingly being reintegrated into their families, women are increasingly leaving them, finding ways of defining themselves that are not exclusively focused around the expressive functions of housewife and mother.

Thus there is another profound change affecting the family in which househusbands are intimately involved: not only are men becoming increasingly reintegrated in their families, but their wives are becoming increasingly disengaged. At least as revolutionary as the reversal of the trend started with the industrial revolution is the rapid erosion of the sexual division of labor. In a remarkably short period of time, the difference between men's work and women's work, surely one of the oldest distinctions in human social history, has become less and less clear. There are those who applaud this revolutionary change and those who deplore it. Although I think that it has both good and bad effects on the lives of men and women, I prefer not to pass judgment on it here — my judgment would not affect it one way or the other anyway — but to point out some of the problems it raises, for social science in general and perhaps for the family itself.

It is a well-accepted sociological axiom that social structures become more stable to the extent that they have a highly developed division of labor. Emile Durkheim pointed this out long ago: a primitive society has a very low division of labor, and hence has little in the way of large-scale institutions. The only institution of primitive society that is stable is the family and tribal extensions of it, precisely the institutions in which there is a division of labor by age and sex. Societies that have greater degrees of specialization — priests, warriors, craftsmen, farmers, administrators — develop larger and more stable institutions. The principal reason why societies with a great deal of specialization are more stable is that people are more interdependent. The greater the division of labor, the greater the degree of interdependence, and the greater stability a social institution has. This cohesion is what Durkheim called "organic solidarity," a solidarity that resembles the mutual interaction of parts of an organism. Modern society, in particular the contemporary

United States, has literally thousands of occupational specialties. The division of labor in such a society is extensive; there is
great interdependence and great organic solidarity, although
social scientists realize that functional interdependence does
not necessarily give people a sense of community and common
identity. In fact, in some ways the division of labor is socially de-
structive, because it isolates people from one another, depriving
them of common experience and a common sense of social
membership. In any case, in much of social life, the division of
labor is increasing, and as our technology becomes more complex, more and more occupational specialties appear. For good
or for ill, specialization is growing, in advanced societies as well
as modernizing ones.

What are we to make of the erosion of the sexual division of
labor inside and outside of the home? To say that it is unexpected, that it flies in the face of trends which for long had been accepted as inescapable by social scientists, is true enough, but
prompts us to go farther: what is this reversal likely to mean for
the stability of the family? At the same time as the rest of society is becoming increasingly specialized, the family is becoming
less and less specialized. The areas of men's and women's work
inside the home are becoming indistinct, as the evidence
reviewed in this book makes clear. In the very deepest sense of
the term, this is an anomaly, a paradoxical development that at
the very least reminds us that theorizing and predicting about
human social behavior is a very risky business indeed. Simply
put, the tendency toward increasing division of labor is not an
inescapable rule.

If an institution is more stable to the extent that it has a greater division of labor, what do these changes mean for the future
stability of the family? At first glance, it does not look promis-
ing. The rate of divorce is increasing; more and more women
are raising children without their fathers or other men being
present; children are increasingly members of families where
their siblings are half-brothers and half-sisters, stepsisters and
stepbrothers. But it would probably be a mistake to blame the
current instability of the nuclear family on the decline in the
sexual division of labor in the home. It probably is much more
closely linked to the erosion of the sexual division of labor outside the home—women free to earn their living are less hesitant
to divorce than those who are entirely dependent on their hus-

bands—and to the long-term change in the basis of marriage from an economic to an emotional one. There are probably even more reasons besides these for the instability of the nuclear family today, but the increase in men's involvement in child care and housework is not one of them. Househusbands may increase the stability of a family by reinforcing the sense of fairness, reciprocity, and egalitarianism, which in turn is the basis for much emotional satisfaction.

We are faced with a violation of the expectations regarding the division of labor that had been shared by generations of social scientists. Not only is the decline in the sexual division of labor in the family going against the prevailing trend, it does not seem to produce an unstable family, and may even increase the stability of the family. A social institution that is going in a direction opposed to that of others in the society, and one in which a decline in the division of labor does not lead to instability, is a scientific surprise. It certainly merits scrutiny over time: the long-term effects on the family of men's taking over substantial amounts of child care and other household tasks needs to be studied, for they are crucial to the future of the family itself.

HOUSEHUSBANDS AND THE QUALITY OF WORK

Two themes that have recurred in this book are the inflexibility of many men's work time and the redeeming characteristics of housework, its concreteness and immediacy. These two ideas are closely related, and to explain how they are linked to househusbands and the quality of work, I will make a brief digression to provide a sketch of two fundamental ideas about the nature of work in modern society: alienation and professionalization.

One of the oldest complaints about the quality of work in modern society is that it is alienated labor. Developed initially by Hegel, the critique of alienation was the intellectual spearhead of the young Marx's attack on capitalism. It is still an idea of which Marxists are inordinately fond, but many non-Marxists have come to accept much of the argument, even as thinkers are coming to realize that alienation is at least as widespread in socialist and communist as in capitalist societies.

Alienation, literally, is a disconnectedness, a lack of connection between people and between themselves and their work.

Marx argued that the worker in capitalist society exchanges his labor power for wages, and is thereby robbed of the creativity that is essentially human. Alienation dehumanizes the worker because instead of creating something, he carries out repetitive work with machinery, creating commodities that belong to someone else. In this situation, man becomes an extension of the machine, rather than the other way around. This estrangement from his labor is intensified by the division of labor, particularly in the assembly line, in which a worker produces only a very small part of a finished product. Not only does his product not belong to him, he has no sense of accomplishment, because he does not create something from beginning to end. He simply pours his labor into making a small part of something and in exchange receives wages. Robbed of any outlet for his creative powers, the only way in which the worker in capitalist society can express himself is through purchasing products; he lives in a "cash nexus," in which relationships are purely monetary and in which his only mode of self-expression is through spending. This produces an obsession with buying products which, in Marx's quaint terminology, is called "commodity fetishism," but which can readily be recognized as a whole pattern of consumerism that is as evident in communist as capitalist society. The alienated worker, in short, simply uses work as a means to an end; it is not creative in the slightest; it is a discomfort, to be exchanged for wages, which in turn are used to buy products. This, in its barest outlines, is the criticism of the alienation of modern society as originally presented by Hegel and Marx.

The perspective I have gained from my years of househusbanding, and the evidence revealed in the survey I conducted, lead me to the conclusion that housework is the last bastion of nonalienated work in modern society. In no other realm of work, save, perhaps, that of the artist or craftsman, are people surrounded by the products of their labor. The tools of their labor belong to them. The fruits of their toil belong to them. Their machines are extensions of themselves, rather than the other way around. Work does not follow the implacable rhythm of the assembly line. There are some rigidities, of course: few demands are as implacable as a crying infant at 3 o'clock in the morning. But these are demands imposed by other people, loved ones, not by an industrial system, for profit.

I am quite aware that this is the opposite of the conventional wisdom among feminists about household work. Wanting to demonstrate as many ways as possible in which women are oppressed, they see housework as a kind of slavery (see, e.g., Schechter, 1978). The most frequent argument is that housework is unpaid work, and that it must be rationalized and made subject to the same procedures as industrial production. As for housework being unpaid work, this is quite obviously untrue — housewives receive remuneration in many forms, including food, clothing, shelter, amusements, amenities, and considerable discretionary power in the spending of household money. It would be more accurate to say that housework is not subject to wage payment. In recognition of this, some feminists have waged a campaign for housewives to be paid wages. But what would this gain, particularly in the light of our observations about alienation? Such a step—making a housewife or househusband into a wage worker would mean simply putting her or him into the same alienated condition as other workers in modern society. If housework were to be "industrialized," how would this be a step forward? It would be simply removing people from one of their few opportunities to be creative, to surround themselves with objects they have conceived of and brought into being. Household work is the last area of preindustrial craft work that we have left. It would, in my opinion, be a drastic mistake to "rationalize" it. Instead, housework, particularly the areas in which people can be creative, as in cooking, child care, and decoration, should be held up and praised as a way of escaping the estrangement to which many are subject in modern life. From my personal experience, I know that it is a pleasant antidote to many of the more inhuman aspects of work outside the home, and many of the househusbands interviewed feel the same way.

Of course, there are studies attesting to the *subjective* alienation of the housewife (see, e.g., Nelson, 1977). How can this be explained? First, psychological measures of alienation are only roughly related to the condition described by Marx and Hegel. These emotions would best be described as *feelings* of estrangement, not the same thing. Alienation is a condition that does not necessarily produce a standard set of emotions; it is an essentially existential condition, and psychologists are simply heading in the wrong direction in trying to quantify and measure it. Second, in a society where virtually all employment is paid with wages or salaries, it is highly likely that the unsung practitioners of nonalienated labor should feel isolated. Artists and other bohemians typically feel this marginality because their work is not paid by wages, and their isolation produces a kind of creative community of the estranged (see, e.g., Grana, 1964). Housewives and househusbands have much in common with the bohemian, working as they all do on the fringes of the salaried work world, doing labor that is simultaneously indispensible and often downgraded. It would be no more progressive to make housewives or househusbands into wage workers than it would to make writers or sculptors into wage workers: little would be gained, and much would be lost.

Rather, what must be done is to rationalize the noncreative aspects of housework, and to encourage more and more men to become involved in its creative aspects. As for the former, this is already happening. The needs of dual career families have created a demand for a wide range of labor-saving technology in the home that is being created and marketed—everything from no-wax floors to disposable diapers and drip-dry clothing.

In Chapter V, we looked at some steps that can be taken to make men freer to become involved in the creative aspects of household work—values are changing, laws can and eventually will be changed, and work policies have already been reshaped in many places of employment. But there is a kind of change under way in the world of work that is making this evolution increasingly possible for men: the professionalization of more and more occupations.

There is a vast body of literature on professionalization (e.g., Freidson, 1977; Vollmer and Mills, 1966). I will summarize here only the essentials of this trend and what they mean for househusbands, alienation, and the world of work. Prior to the industrial revolution, manufacturing was organized by craft. A craftsman worked essentially alone, helped perhaps by an apprentice or a journeyman. After the industrial revolution, work came to be organized in a very different way. It was collective, there was a chain of command, a hierarchy of wages and power. In a word, work was organized bureaucratically. Each task was broken down into its simplest parts, and carried out by workers taking orders from above. Industrial work is organized in a paramilitary fashion. Perhaps most important, little skill was needed in the typical industrial enterprise, because work was extensively "rationalized" and simplified. One could learn a job in fifteen minutes, and carry out simple, repetitive tasks as long as ordered to. This is the world of alienated labor, so justly criticized for its inhumanity and dullness.

Since the beginning of the twentieth century, however, a new mode of work organization has developed. Technological progress reduced the number of manual workers required for industrial production; the proportion of blue-collar workers has been steadily declining in industrial societies, and the proportion of unskilled workers among them has diminished to a tiny few. Marx's industrial proletariat, that mass of ragged expeasants with nothing to live by but the sale of their raw labor power, has almost vanished from the work forces of advanced industrial societies.

What has taken its place? White-collar workers, some of whom are highly skilled and some of whom are hardly skilled at all. Among the skilled white-collar workers, more and more are becoming professional. Professionalization consists, basically, of the following characteristics: a professional learns how to do his job in an institution separated from his job, usually an institution of higher learning; he becomes legally qualified to practice his profession by dint of this specialized training; he belongs to a professional association whose job it is to establish and maintain professional ethics, to monopolize and expand the area in which the professionals may exclusively operate, to accredit or disenfranchise the schools that train the professionals and to maintain control over the quality of persons admitted to the profession. Most important, the professional does not work according to instructions given him by others; the professional does his work according to a set of inner demands, those of excellence, competence, and professional ethics. More and more occupations are becoming professionalized: in addition to the classic professions of law and medicine, there are newer ones, such as engineering, teaching, social work, accounting, and a host of others. In the same way that the white-collar workers displaced the blue-collar workers because of the development of labor-saving technology in the factory, the professional is displacing the semi-skilled white-collar workers because of the development of labor-saving technology in the office. More and more of the routine jobs of a bureaucracy can be carried out by computer. The computer is eliminating the necessity for more and more of the traditional white-collar jobs, and the work force is being transformed into a series of professionals whose relation to their work is entirely different from that of the craftsman or the industrial worker. Professionals are not only less alienated, they have much more freedom to shape their time as they see fit. This is where the convergences among househusbands, alienation, and professionalization develop. As more and more jobs become professionalized, more and more men and women will have freer time to become reinvolved with their families. Professionalization is clearly linked to degree of househusbanding, as this and other studies have shown, and we can expect that more and more men will become househusbands to the extent that their occupations are professionalized.

Professionalization of occupations is accompanied by another major factor that will help the reintegration of men into their families: the computer and communications revolutions. As more and more jobs are being done by computer, more people can afford to have their computers at home. The development of microcircuits and miniaturization has made it feasible for a computer to be as natural a part of a home's furnishing as a television set and a telephone. This home computer can easily be linked up with a company computer by telephone, so that more jobs can be done at home. Increasingly, professionals are doing much of their work on their computers at home, visiting their offices perhaps once or twice a week to pick up work and confer with colleagues. Journalistic accounts of this profound change in work structures are beginning to appear (see, e.g., *Newsweek*, 1981), but only the outlines of its implications for the family are apparent now.

What appears to be happening is a reversion to the home-based work of the preindustrial age, and the househusbands we have studied are among the forerunners of this trend. The craftsman or peasant worked essentially at home, and so will the professional whose home computer is linked by telephone to his company computer. If the industrial revolution separated men from their families because it concentrated capital in order to make more efficient production possible, what we are seeing now is a kind of decentralization of capital. The professional of the future—and more and more workers will be professionals—will be occupied in a kind of computerized cottage industry. Work will no longer be collective and subject to forced industrial rhythms; it will be increasingly like that of the artisan, much more solitary than industrial work, and, most important of all, will be done at home. The trends of professionalization and computerization will mean that more and more men and women can work in the company of one another and their families. The radical separation of home and work will be gradually abolished. Because of professionalization, work will be less alienated; even when work is alienating the concrete and immediate world of child care and cooking will offer men and women an antidote. But most important of all, men, who have been so cruelly separated from their homes by the exigencies of industrialism, will be returning to their wives and children.

CONCLUSION

All the factors indicate that the number of equal time and full-time househusbands will increase in the United States. Employment of wives outside the home, changing values regarding appropriate behavior for men, changing policies regarding work time, changes in the legal system, the growth of professionalism, the computer and communications revolutions—all promise to encourage the reintegration of men into their families and their increasing acceptance of responsibility for household tasks. The evidence we have seen from the interviews with househusbands shows that on the whole the experience is positive for men and their families.

Men seem to take over substantial amounts of housework with remarkable pragmatism, lack of self-consciousness, and even lack of fanfare, in spite of what might be expected about men and housework from common (and frequently untested) assumptions about the roles appropriate to men in American society. I must confess that this was not particularly surprising to me, because my own experience with housework over the last five years has been, on the whole, similarly rewarding rather than burdensome. The evidence also shows that many men actually like housework, which was certainly unexpected. As a sociologist I may be chastened to find that many assumptions sacred to the profession are seemingly so incorrect. But as a family man I am encouraged by this for two reasons: first, sex roles may not be the straightjackets they are often depicted to be, but are more like the lines in a parking lot that tell people where to park their cars. Most people park their cars in the slots as indicated, but occasionally a free spirit will take up two spaces or park diagonally. What is more important is that the lines can be redrawn, and in the case of men doing housework, the redrawing of the lines is not as deeply traumatic an experience as might be expected. And in the light of the evidence that men doing housework can promote family solidarity, this bodes well for the family.

A leading feminist once said, "A woman needs a man like a fish needs a bicycle." Fortunately for the human race, she is wrong. Men and women need each other, particularly in family life, with its myriad kinds of interdependence. Instead of increasing the estrangement of men and women from each other, the growing numbers of househusbands foreshadow growing cooperation between the sexes in the family, that most fundamental of human institutions.

Appendix A:
An Explanation of the Method Used in the Househusbands Survey

This book is an attempt to combine two types of sociological research, the analytical and the descriptive. Descriptive sociological research simply tries to tell people what is there, primarily because little or no attention has been previously paid to it. Analytical sociological research tries to establish causal relationships and to fit these relationships into a general theoretical system. In the latter endeavor, it is no different from any other science, and mainstream sociologists use the same techniques. Hypothetical relationships are extracted from the existing body of theory and tested against empirical reality. If the hypotheses are confirmed, the theory is considered validated, whereas, if the hypothesis is disconfirmed, the theory is revised according to the new evidence. Of course, it is never as simple and straightforward as this; this image of scientific research is part of the description of what Thomas Kuhn (1970) calls "normal science" that is false, and covers up the accidents, the equivocations, the ideological struggles, and occasional outright dishonesty that take place in scientific research.

Descriptive sociological research can use either of the two major sociological research methods, the case study or the survey. A great deal of survey research that is purely descriptive is on the order of public opinion polls, in which little attempt is made to study causal relations. But all analytical research must use the survey method, because without its mathematical precision, it is extremely difficult to make assertions about systematic relations between variables. My questionnaire attempts to combine the depth yielded by a case study—in which a great deal is discovered about relatively few people—and the breadth and precision yielded by the survey —

which finds out a relatively small amount of information about a large number of people. A critic might say that it has the weaknesses of both: the case study suffers from the fact that researchers do not know whether the case or cases they are looking at are in any way representative, and hence can only generalize with difficulty. And the survey suffers from the fact that living, breathing people are reduced to mathematical relationships between variables, and one is never sure that all the variables have been taken into account. Such a criticism would be correct, except that the peculiar nature of househusbands would make systematic generalization about them difficult at this time, and the fact that so little has been written about them that the field of sex role research is in real need of in-depth inquiries about men in family life.

SAMPLING PROCEDURE AND SAMPLE

In orthodox survey research, hypotheses are translated into variables that are included in questions on a standard questionnaire. This questionnaire is then administered to the group of people among whom the causal relationships suggested in the hypothesis are supposed to apply. The practical problem, of course, is that theory, by its nature, purports to apply to a very large group of people. The fact is that it is practically impossible (except for the government), to administer a questionnaire to an entire population, and a sample of a population must be established in which the questionnaire is administered. Measures must be taken to make sure that the sample is representative of the population, so that what one says of a thousand or so people is applicable to millions. Elaborate statistical procedures are used to set up and test samples for their representativeness.

When I first started thinking of doing a survey of househusbands, I became aware that this procedure was impossible. Since so little has been written about men and housework, there was no way to find out the characteristics of the population within which I was trying to test my hypotheses and whose general characteristics I was trying to describe. I therefore decided purposely to restrict my sample to a relatively homogeneous group, in order to eliminate some of the variables that could make for significant differences among househusbands.

The first variable I decided to control was race. There are significant differences in family structure and sex roles between whites and blacks, Hispanics, Orientals, and other minorities conventionally considered to be nonwhite. Not, of course, that these men are not important; but in order to eliminate the variation that their presence would introduce, I had to make the sample all white. The next variable to control had to be country of socialization. Men who have been born outside the United States and have spent even a small portion of their boyhoods in other cultures are shaped by other sex roles; they differ significantly from those found in the United States. My second criterion was therefore that the respondents had to have been born and raised in the United States. This is not a perfect control, of course. First-generation Americans may differ from seventh-generation Americans, but respondents' generation of immigration would have proved impractical to control.

Just as important as variables associated with race and culture, I believed were the circumstances under which men found themselves doing household tasks. Two male roommates doing laundry or a man cooking for himself are not examples of househusbandry, because it is the reciprocity of the role that is important, particularly as it involves changing expectations and performance between the sexes. I therefore decided that a female adult had to be present in the household, either as wife or as cohabitant, because it was the division of labor with her that was important. Similarly, the presence of at least one child was required of respondents, because the presence of a child not only geometrically increases the quantity of the housework to be done, but calls out the conventional sex-role expectations that a woman is the chief agent in child care; men who were taking over significant portions of child care were not only doing quantitatively more housework but housework that was, qualitatively, extremely different from the norm as well.

In sum, the 56 men who are studied in this report are white, American-born, and living with or married to a woman in a household with at least one child present. The sample may not be representative of all men who have partially or entirely taken over household tasks, but this group is so heterogeneous that extensive generalization about it at present would not be fruitful anyway.

There are several justifications besides the practical for having compiled my sample in such an unorthodox way. First, having set up a homogeneous sample like this, I feel that within these limits (with some educational, occupational, and religious variations that can be taken into account), there is a fairly consistent definition of what the male sex role is. As I pointed out in the Introduction, my main interest was in finding out the reactions of men to carrying on activities on a sustained basis that were not in accordance with conventional expectations. Among white, American-born men who have a child and a wife in their households, there is a fairly consistent set of role expectations, particularly concerning the division of work in the home. And I expected that the homogeneity of the sample would make it possible to generalize about other men's reactions to housework, to the extent that they do it. In short, I am generalizing on the basis of a small sample because of the consistency of role expectations of men in the population at large.

In addition, many other social scientists have used the technique of small, selected samples to map out unexplored territory. Freud's sample of patients was not at all representative, but this did not prevent him from erecting one of the greatest theories of human personality and development in existence. Sex researchers such as Kinsey and Masters and Johnson also have felt safe in generalizing about populations on the basis of samples that were far from random. And finally, in the area of the sociology of housework, Ann Oakley's sample was selected rather than random; I feel fairly safe in having used the same data-gathering technique as one of the pioneers in the sociology of housework.

HOW THE RESPONDENTS WERE LOCATED

The respondents were located by means of three methods: from a list of respondents to another, similar survey; from advertisements in newspapers; and from referrals given by other respondents. David Lutwin, a doctoral candidate at the New York University School of Social Work, compiled a sample of househusbands while preparing his dissertation on the subject. One of his methods was to seek respondents by means of an advertisement in the *Village Voice*. I responded to this advertisement and asked him if I could send my questionnaire to his sample. He very graciously agreed, and we arranged for him to send the questionnaires, without identifying the respondents to me, to guarantee confidentiality. Only about twenty of his sample responded—many had moved, their mail not forwardable—and of these only four fit all the criteria I had established for my sample. Nonetheless, I am grateful to Mr. Lutwin for his cooperation.

My main technique for finding respondents was by advertisements. I had tried advertising in the *Village Voice* and the *New York Review of Books* during a pilot study, with meager results. I therefore decided to use advertisements in local Brooklyn newspapers (*Phoenix, Flatbush Life, Canarsie Courier, Sheepshead Bay News,* and *Starrett City News*). I made this decision in hopes of getting both more respondents and a more heterogeneous mix than the relatively unrepresentative readership of the *New York Review of Books* or the *Village Voice.* The following advertisement appeared weekly for five weeks:

MEN AND HOUSEWORK

Research project seeks men who have partially or entirely taken over household tasks such as cooking, cleaning, child care and household maintenance. Please call 780-5314 or write "Men and Housework," Department of Sociology, Brooklyn College, Brooklyn, New York 11210.

The address was provided to identify the research project as legitimate to prospective respondents. The advertisements produced scores of respondents, but many did not fit the criteria spelled out above. At the end of the questionnaire the respondent is asked to identify any other men he knows who have also taken over household tasks. If they qualified, questionnaires were administered to them as well.

INTERVIEW SETTING

With the exception of the four respondents who were sent their questionnaires by mail for them to fill out (and one who is employed at Brooklyn College), all subjects were interviewed at home. Because of the possibility of bias, they were interviewed alone, in the absence of spouse or female cohabitant. The presence of such a person would be likely to influence responses either in the direction of a man's overstating or understating his share of housework, and certainly would be likely to influence his answers to the open-ended questions near the end of the questionnaire. The interviewer was male, since I also realized that a female interviewer would be likely to lead the respondent to change his answers in some ways according to perceived expectations on the part of the interviewer.

The entire interview was recorded and later transcribed. The open-ended questions quoted in the text above are verbatim, with the only excisions being personal names and occasionally other items that could identify the respondents. Strict confidentiality was promised and maintained.

THE QUESTIONNAIRE

Within this homogeneous, selected sample, in-depth interviews asking both precoded and open-ended questions were conducted, using a nine-page questionnaire with 57 items. A facsimile of the questionnaire is found in Appendix B. The reader will see that many questions were asked that produced data not analyzed in this book, which was intended for a relatively unspecialized readership. Further publications will use those data that were not discussed in this study.

The questionnaire was based on a modification of an instrument used in a pretest by a research seminar given in fall 1978 in the Brooklyn College Department of Sociology. Most of the questions that appear on the final questionnaire were used in the pretest. There were three main changes: the technique for measuring shares of housework done, the omission of a test on self-definition, and the addition of questions relating to power in the family.

In the original instrument, the following question was used to ascertain the division of household labor: "Would you please indicate about which proportion of the following tasks you do?"

(Please circle one in each row.)	none at all	less than half	share equally	more than half	do entirely
Child care (feeding, bathing, dressing, changing diapers)	0	1	2	3	4
Cooking	0	1	2	3	4
Shopping for food and other household items	0	1	2	3	4
Washing dishes and pots	0	1	2	3	4
Laundry	0	1	2	3	4
Cleaning house (dusting vacuuming floors, waxing, etc.)	0	1	2	3	4

The same question was used to establish the proportions of housework carried out by the respondent's father and by his wife or cohabitant. This apparently symmetrical question, I soon found, concealed more than it revealed, because men who did some 5 percent of a job and men who did 45 percent of a job were both classified as doing "less than half" of it. Because of the lack of precision of this question, a more detailed but more cumbersome and time-consuming format was adopted.

A self-definition question was used, a modification of the Kuhn and McPartland Twenty Statements Test (Kuhn and McPartland, 1964), to try to measure the extent of men's tendency to make "consensual" or "subconsensual" statements about themselves. In Kuhn and McPartland's terms, these mean, respectively, a tendency to identify oneself in group-identity terms or affective, qualitative terms. I wanted to ask this question for two reasons. First, Oakley had used a Ten Statements Test in her study of housewives in London, and I wanted to compare her results with mine. Second, I was interested in the effects of housework on men both because I wanted to see if it changed them in any significant way from the norm, and because I wanted to see if househusbands were integrated into their roles. Men tend to given consensual rather than subconsensual statements, and it would have been interesting to see if my respondents had a lesser tendency to do so. As for role-integration, basic role theory postulates that there will be role conflict if a person is carrying out a role that he or she has not internalized. If househusbands tended to identify more in terms of their family activity than nonhousehusbands, then I would have been able to offer an optimistic prognosis about the future stability of such men and the families in which they functioned.

Unfortunately, the test had to be abandoned because of difficulties in interpreting the data and because causality could not be established. It was extremely difficult clearly to differentiate, on the basis of the pretests, between the two types of statements, and even if it had been possible, it would not be clear whether this atypical self-identification by a respondent was the result of doing housework or the factor that led the respondent to take over the tasks in the first place.

The questions relating to power and health practices were added at the end, to replicate another study, as explained later in this Appendix.

An explanation of the protocol of questions used follows; some of these are relatively straightforward, but some require explanation as to their purpose and how they were used to correspond to variables to test hypotheses.

Questions 1 and 2 ask the name and address of the respondent. Aside from identification for my own purposes, the principal reason for asking these questions is a follow-up study I plan to carry out in five years, which will consist of a mailed questionnaire that will attempt to find out how the division of labor in the homes has changed, if at all, and how the respondents' attitudes have changed toward family work, work outside the home, themselves, and their spouses or cohabitants.

Independent Variables

In general, questions 3-37 and questions 42 and 43 were thought of as independent variables, factors which in the framework of this study could be thought of as having an effect on such phenomena as reactions to housework and how the housework affected respondent's relations to outside work and other people and his feelings about himself.

Question 3 asks year of birth to ascertain the variable of age.

Question 4 asks if the respondent was born in the United States. The primary purpose of this question was to confirm that the respondent answered the criterion of being American-born, in case he had been misunderstood during the telephone conversation that set up the interview.

Question 5 asks if the respondent is employed outside the

home; question 6 offers five alternative answers to a question for those who answer "no" to question 5 (unemployed, retired, disabled, at home by choice, or other). The purpose of question 6 is to differentiate those men who are not employed outside the home because of circumstances beyond their control from those who have chosen to be at home.

For those who answered "yes" to question 5, question 7 established respondent's occupation. This response was written in longhand by the interviewer, and a three-digit code was assigned later, during the coding of the interview. The *Dictionary of Occupational Titles* (U.S. Department of Labor, 1977) was used to assign this three-digit code.

For those who answered "yes" to question 5, question 8 establishes whether the respondent is employed full time or outside.

Questions 9-11 establish the number of children living in the home, their sex, and their ages.

The purpose of question 12 was similar to that of question 4, to ensure that the respondent answered the criteria of the selected sample, in case a misunderstanding had occurred during the telephone conversation that had set up the interview appointment.

Question 13 ascertains whether the female counterpart is employed outside the home.

For those who answer "no" to question 13, question 14 asks for the same set of alternative responses offered in question 6, to establish if the woman is at home by choice or through circumstances that are beyond her control.

Question 14 establishes the occupation of the female counterparts who are employed outside the home; the same procedure was used for coding the responses to this question as for question 7.

Question 16's purpose is to find out if those female counterparts employed outside the home work full time or part time.

Questions 17-20 find out if there are any other adult females or males living in the household, and what their relationship is to the respondent or the respondent's female counterpart. Such adults, I realized, would be likely to play a significant part in the division of household labor.

Question 21, like questions 12 and 5, controlled the selection of white respondents for inclusion in the sample.

Question 22 asked the respondent's religious affiliation in

order to control for this variable when tabulating responses to questions about reactions to housework, as well as for possible serendipitous revelations when tabulating responses to other variables. I thought that there might be significant variation in sex-role expectations in different religious groups.

The reason for asking question 23, regarding self-identification by ethnic group, was the same as for question 22. This response was not pre-coded, as ethnicity is a more plastic and variable status than race or religion, and I wanted to have as much room for freedom and variety in the response as possible; for this reason, two digits were allowed in the coding. Responses were subsequently coded on the basis of identical responses.

Question 24 elicits the level of education of the respondent, as this variable was seen as one of the most important in determining variations in sex-role expectations for men.

Questions 25-30 aim to find out if the respondent had a full set of male and female role models during his childhood, either in the form of a biological parent, a grandparent, or a stepparent.

Question 31 asks whether the respondent's father was employed outside the home for most of respondent's childhood. Its purpose is to make it possible, when analyzing the other data, to differentiate between men whose male role models were fulfilling the conventional role of a father working outside the home. "Most of" a respondent's childhood was meant to elicit the *memory* of the subject, which was thought to be the important element for a model.

The purpose of question 32 was similar, to differentiate for those who answered "no" to question 31, between respondents whose fathers were at home by choice, were employed at home, or were at home because of circumstances beyond their control.

For those whose fathers were employed outside the home, question 33 asks what his occupation was or is; the response was coded in the same fashion as those to questions 7 and 15. I thought that this would be a variable potentially as important as the respondent's occupation, because the social class in which a person is socialized often has a lasting effect, sometimes more important than occupational status.

Question 34 asks if the respondent's mother was employed

outside the home for most of his childhood, according to his recollection, because I anticipated that this might have an effect on the man's point of view of the appropriate role for his female counterpart. A man whose mother was a full-time housewife might have a different view than other men of the domestic role of women, based on his memory of his mother's role.

The purpose of question 35 was similar; if the respondent's mother was at home by choice, her demonstration of what was appropriate for women at home would be different from that of a mother who was at home in spite of her wishes.

For those whose mothers were employed outside the home, question 36 establishes what her occupation was; the responses were coded as for questions 7, 15, and 33.

Question 37 attempts to ascertain the division of labor in the household in which the respondent was socialized. The pretest of the questionnaire revealed that questions asking general recollections regarding the division of labor along broad lines did not yield information that was sufficiently detailed to get a clear picture of all the aspects of household work. A standard list of household jobs taken from Karen Geiken (1964) was adapted for use on this questionnaire. It is meant not to be an exhaustive list of all of the aspects of work in the home, but to give a reasonable picture of the scope of the tasks involved, so that respondents can assign the specific amounts of work which, according to their recollections, were done by different members of their families. They were asked to list the approximate number of hours per week spent on the tasks by members of their families: father, mother, and other people, whom they were asked to specify. The total number of hours for the entire family was added up, and the number was divided into the number of hours spent on housework by the father of the family, to obtain a two-digit percentage code.

Perhaps I should emphasize that I did not expect that respondents would have a completely accurate picture of the division of household labor during their childhoods. What is of primary sociological interest is their *recollection* of this, the division of labor in their childhood as it appears to them now, and as it affects their participation in household tasks. Sociologists have a term called "the definition of the situation" to explain how this takes place. People define reality in certain ways and then act upon their definitions. The definition may not be "true" in an objective sense, but this is less important than the fact that it is used as a way of guiding present behavior. In short, men's perceptions of the sexual division of labor in their childhoods is used as a part of their definition of the situation as regards their performance of and reactions to housework.

I anticipated that the responses to this question would be particularly important for testing the importance of the father as role model, whether they confirmed or disconfirmed the hypothesis.

Dependent Variables

Questions 44, 45, 46, 47, 48, and 49 attempt to measure dependent variables, factors that in the context of the study can be thought to be affected by the independent variables explained above.

Before discussing them, a word must be said about question 38. This question attempts to ascertain the division of labor in the respondent's household, using the same method as in question 37. The information elicited by this question was to serve as a dependent variable in some cases, as in the testing of the role-model hypothesis, and as an independent variable in the analysis of questions regarding the respondent's reactions to housework.

Question 43 aims to find out the motivations of the respondent for taking over household tasks. This is an open-ended question, because little could be anticipated with certainty about the types of answers that would be given, and precoded responses would have seriously affected the depth and variety of the answers given. These responses were treated both in their transcribed form, as quoted in the text, and were coded to differentiate between: (1) those respondents whose explanations tended to indicate that their motivation was voluntary, either based on a preference for the work or based on some sort of ideological belief in the equity of the arrangement, and (2) those who indicated no preference but who referred to external circumstances that obliged them to do so, assertions that they had always done them, and similarly preferentially neutral statements. Since these decisions on coding were not always easy to make, the full-length quotations should be used as an indispensable supplement to the quantitative data.

Question 44 asks if the respondent likes housework, in general. The primary purpose of this question is for comparison with the results presented by Oakley (1974). As with question 43, the open-ended questions were coded, in this case to differentiate between responses that indicated that the respondent likes housework, dislikes it, or either does not mind it or has an ambivalent attitude. Again, these coding decisions were not always easy and the answers considerably less than clear-cut, and the responses are quoted as a supplement to the tables.

Questions 45 and 46 are treated as purely open-ended questions and reported in the form of quotes. Aside from informational purposes, these questions were initially in the form: "What would you say are the best things about being a househusband?" and "What would you say are the worst things about being a househusband?" These questions were also designed for comparison with Oakley's survey, in which the questions were asked with regard to being a housewife. But the pretest quickly showed that the term "househusband" was virtually meaningless to most respondents. The wording was accordingly changed, and the question was used for descriptive purposes only.

Questions 47 and 48 ask how the respondent's feelings about himself and his female counterpart have changed since he started doing housework. The purpose of these questions was to find out the effects of changing sex-role performance on a man's conception of himself and on his interaction with a significant female other. The nature of the responses to these questions was necessarily difficult to quantify. In the pretest, I had used the Ten Statements Test (the Twenty Statements Test devised by Kuhn and McPartland, as shortened to ten statements by Oakley). The results, however, were so anomalous that I decided to opt simply for open-ended responses to look at this variable. What is more, even if I had had a more precise measurement of self-conception and other-orientation, it would have been impossible, without a panel survey over time, to find out the direction of causality. In other words, if I found that these househusbands had unusual self-conceptions in comparison to other men, I could not conclude that it was the performance of household tasks that had changed their self-conception; it could very well have been their unusual self-conception that led them to undertake these tasks in the first place. Accordingly, a sort of pseudo-panel question was asked, directing the respondent to assess for himself changes that had taken place over time. True panel surveys are notoriously difficult to carry out, and in the framework of this grant and this project, I had to settle for a pseudopanel, with all its methodological weaknesses.

The same rationale applies to question 49, with reference to changing orientation toward work outside the home. For the conventional American male, for social and legal reasons, work outside the home is his primary status, because of his instrumental function. Because of the variety and heterogeneity of the responses received, this question, too, was not subsequently coded.

Intervening and Other Variables

Questions 39, 40, and 41 were designed to measure intervening variables, which could have some effect between the independent variables and the dependent variables described earlier. The strategy of many dual career families is to use outside services to perform household duties, ranging from laundry service through child care to house cleaning. The families of househusbands are notable exceptions to this, and with these three questions I wanted to find out to what extent the respondents did choose this option, for what services, and why.

As for questions 50-55, they were taken from a study by Lois Pratt (1956) in order to find out how the health-teaching practices of her conventional families compare to the families studied in this survey.

CONCLUSION: CASE STUDY AND SURVEY

The method used in this report combines the case study and survey methods. It is a case study in the sense that it looks in depth at a deliberately restricted sample of respondents. As such, it provides both descriptive and analytical statements about a group of men who participate extensively in housework, but who cannot be proven to be representative of other men who participate extensively in housework, to say nothing of other men who might be put in this situation. It is a survey in the sense that it uses a protocol of questions, which were all administered under similar circumstances; the questions are mostly precoded but also include open-ended questions. Thus,

it has the advantage of standardization that anu
case studies, which tend to use straightforward obsu
participant observation, do not have. At the same time
veals a weakness of the method: for practical as well as fin
reasons, it was impossible for a researcher to spend time
the families of the respondents to observe the process of hou
work over time.

The strengths of the method—standardization and an in-depth study—are enough to support the conclusions reached, and to generate some of the speculations made. Those in search of other types of answers, from large-scale surveys using proba-bility samples, and from participant-observation case studies, must look elsewhere; however, such research does not yet exist in published form.

Appendix B:
Questionnaire Used in the
Househusbands Survey

Questionnaire I.D. No. _____

We greatly appreciate your willingness to participate in this research project. We would like to assure you that your responses to this questionnaire will be kept strictly confidential, and that you are under no obligation to answer the questions.

1. Name _____
                  last   *first*   *initial*

2. Address _____
                  number and street

   _____
       city or town   *state*   *zip*

   (The above information is requested for a follow-up study.)

3. Year of Birth _____
                                    col. 5-6

4. Were you born in the United States? 0-YES 1-NO *(circle one)*
                                    col. 7

5. Are you employed in an occupation outside the home? 0-YES 1-NO
                                    col. 8

6. If NO, are you 0-Unemployed   *(circle one)*
                   1-Retired
                   2-Disabled
                   3-At home by choice
                   4-Other _____
                                 (please specify)   col. 9

7. What is your present occupation, or the last occupation you had outside the home? _____
                              (please be as specific as possible)   col. 10-12

8. If you are presently employed outside the home, please indicate if you are employed 0-FULL TIME or 1-PART TIME.
(circle one)
                                    col. 13

9. How many children are living in your household? *(circle one)*

    0 1 2 3 4 5 more than 5

    col. 14

10. What are the ages of the girls? *(circle as many as apply)*

    0-less than one year 1 2 3 4 5 6 7 8 9 10
    11 12 13 14 15 16 17 18 19 20 21

    col. 15-24

11. What are the ages of the boys? *(circle as many as apply)*

    0-less than one year 1 2 3 4 5 6 7 8 9 10
    11 12 13 14 15 16 17 18 19 20 21

    col. 25-34

12. Is there a woman presently living in the household as wife or cohabitant? 0-YES 1-NO

(circle one)

    col. 35

13. If YES, is she employed outside the home?

0-YES 1-NO   *(circle one)*

    col. 36

14. If NO, is she 0-Unemployed
              1-Retired
              2-Disabled
              3-At home by choice
              4-Other _____

                            (please specify)   col. 37

15. What is her present occupation, or the last occupation she had outside the home? _____

                          (please be as specific as possible)   col. 38-40

16. If she is currently employed outside the home, is she employed
0-FULL TIME or 1-PART TIME

    col. 41

17. Are the any other adult females living in your household?
    0-YES 1-NO

    col. 42

18. If YES, what is her relationship? 0-Your mother
                              1-Your wife's/partner's mother
18a. (If NO, write 9 in col. 43)   2-Your grandmother
                              3-Wife's/partner's grandmother
                              4-Other _____

                            (please specify)   col. 43

19. Are the any other adult males living in your household?
    0-YES 1-NO

    col. 44

20. If YES, what is his relationship? 0-Your father
                             1-Your wife's/partner's father
20a. (If NO, write 9 in col. 45)   2-Your grandfather
                              3-Wife's/partner's grandfather
                              4-Other _____

                            (please specify)   col. 45

21. How would you classify yourself by race?

    0   1   2   3   4
    BLACK WHITE ORIENTAL NATIVE AMERICAN OTHER _____
                (circle one)   *(please specify*   col. 46

22. How would you classify yourself by religion?

      0   1   2   3

    CATHOLIC JEWISH PROTESTANT OTHER _____

               (circle one)   *(please specify*   col. 47

23. Some Americans identify themselves as members of ethnic groups (such as Italian-Americans, Irish-Americans, or Chicanos). If you identify yourself in this way, which ethnic group do you belong to?

    _____

24. We are interested in how much education you have had. What is the highest level of education you have achieved?

0-less than high school diploma	4-some graduate school	*(circle*
1-high school diploma	5-technical degree	*highest*
2-some college	6-Master's degree	*level*
3-college degree (BA or BS)	7-doctorate, law degree, or MD	

         col. 50

25. When you were growing up, were both your mother and father present in the household for most of your childhood?

    0-YES 1-NO   *(circle one)*

         col. 51

26. If NO, which were absent?

    0-MOTHER 1-FATHER 2-BOTH *(circle one)*   col. 52

27. If your MOTHER was deceased or otherwise absent, was there another woman living in the household? 0-YES 1-NO

    (If mother not deceased, write 9 in col. 53)   col. 53

28. If YES, what was her relationship? 0-stepmother

               (circle one)   1-grandmother

                            2-Other _____

                                    (please specify)   col. 54

29. If your FATHER was deceased or otherwise absent, was there another man living in the household? 0-YES 1-NO

    (If father not deceased, write 9 in col. 55)   col. 55

30. If YES, what was his relationship? 0-stepfather

               (circle one)   1-grandfather

                            2-Other _____

    30a. (If NO, write 9 in col. 56)   *(please specify)*   col. 56

31. When you were growing up, was your father employed outside the home for most of your childhood?

    0-YES 1-NO   *(circle one)*

         col. 57

32. If NO, was he 0-Unemployed

32a. (If YES,   1-Retired

        write 9 in   2-Disabled

        col. 58)   3-At home by choice

                    Other _____

                                  (please specify)   col. 58

33. If YES, what was his occupation? _____

33a. (If NO, write 999 in col. 59-61) *(please be as specific as possible)*   col.59-61

34. When you were growing up, was your mother employed outside the home for most of your childhood?
0-YES 1-NO *(circle one)*

col. 62

35. If NO, was he 0-Unemployed
35a. (If YES,   1-Retired
write 9 in   2-Disabled
col. 63)   3-At home by choice
Other _____

(please specify) col. 63

36. If YES, what was her occupation? _____
33a. (If NO, write 999 in col. 64-66) *(please be as specific as possible)* col.64-66

37. We are interested in how household work was divided up in your home when you were a child. Here is a list of household tasks. About how many hours per week were spent on each of these tasks by your mother, your father or some other person?

FATHER   MOTHER   PERSON #1   PERSON #2

____ ____ ____ ____ Doing the weekly grocery shopping
____ ____ ____ ____ Entertaining the children in late afternoon & evening
____ ____ ____ ____ Bathing and dressing the children
____ ____ ____ ____ Feeding the children
____ ____ ____ ____ Doing the laundry
____ ____ ____ ____ Spending time with the boys in the family
____ ____ ____ ____ Preparing the meals
____ ____ ____ ____ Doing the vacuuming
____ ____ ____ ____ Staying home with the children part of the weekend
____ ____ ____ ____ Doing the ironing
____ ____ ____ ____ Doing the dusting
____ ____ ____ ____ Guiding the children's play activities
____ ____ ____ ____ Keeping clothes in repair
____ ____ ____ ____ Scrubbing and waxing floors
____ ____ ____ ____ Spending time with the girls in the family
____ ____ ____ ____ Drying the dishes
____ ____ ____ ____ Washing dishes
____ ____ ____ ____ Babysitting in the evenings
____ ____ ____ ____ Washing windows
____ ____ ____ ____ Shopping for clothes for the children
____ ____ ____ ____ Gardening or other yard work
____ ____ ____ ____ TOTAL

$$\frac{\text{TOTAL FATHER'S HOURS}}{\text{TOTAL HOURS}} = \underline{\quad}$$

col. 67-68

38. We are interested in how household work was divided up in your household today. Here is a list of the same household tasks. About how many hours per week are spent on each of these tasks by yourself, your wife/cohabitant or some other person?

SELF	WIFE	PERSON #1	PERSON #2	
————	————	————	————	Doing the weekly grocery shopping
————	————	————	————	Entertaining the children in late afternoon & evening
————	————	————	————	Bathing and dressing the children
————	————	————	————	Feeding the children
————	————	————	————	Doing the laundry
————	————	————	————	Spending time with the boys in the family
————	————	————	————	Preparing the meals
————	————	————	————	Doing the vacuuming
————	————	————	————	Staying home with the children part of the weekend
————	————	————	————	Doing the ironing
————	————	————	————	Doing the dusting
————	————	————	————	Guiding the children's play activities
————	————	————	————	Keeping clothes in repair
————	————	————	————	Scrubbing and waxing floors
————	————	————	————	Spending time with the girls in the family
————	————	————	————	Drying the dishes
————	————	————	————	Washing dishes
————	————	————	————	Babysitting in the evenings
————	————	————	————	Washing windows
————	————	————	————	Shopping for clothes for the children
————	————	————	————	Gardening or other yard work
————	————	————	————	TOTAL

$$\frac{\text{TOTAL R'S HOURS}}{\text{TOTAL HOURS}} = \text{————}$$

col. 69-70

39. Apart from an occasional visit to a restaurant or use of a baby sitter, do you regularly use an outside service to perform any of the tasks just listed? 0-YES   1-NO   *(circle one)*

col. 71

40. If YES, which one(s)? _____
40a. (If NO, write 9 in col. 72)   *(please specify)*

col. 72

41. Could you explain briefly why? _____
_____
_____

col. 73

42. Of the tasks that you do, about how long have you been doing these jobs?
0-less than   1   2   3   4   5-more than
   1 year   year   years years years   4 years
              (circle one)

col. 74

43. Why did you take over these tasks? _____
_____
_____
_____

Now we would like to ask some more in-depth questions.

44. Do you like housework, in general? _____
_____
_____
_____

45. What would you say are the best things about housework? _____
_____
_____
_____

46. What would you say are the worst things about housework? _____
_____
_____
_____

47. In what ways do you feel different about yourself since you started doing housework? _____
_____
_____
_____

48. In what ways do you feel different about your wife/cohabitant since you started doing housework? _____
_____
_____
_____

49. In what ways have your feelings about working outside the home changed since you started doing housework? _____
_____
_____
_____

Now we would like to ask some questions relating to health care and health education.

50. For each of the following, please indicate whether or not you have explained to your child about it. *(circle YES or NO)*

    YES NO   The proper way to use a toothbrush
    YES NO   The proper kinds of foods to eat
    YES NO   The effects of smoking on health

YES   NO   When and how much to exercise
YES   NO   How to clean yourself in order to maintain a healthy body
YES   NO   The importance of moving one's bowels regularly
YES   NO   The effect of irregular or lack of sleep upon health
YES   NO   How reproduction takes place between the sexes

51. Have you ever done any of the following things to teach your child(ren) health habits (for example, about brushing teeth, sleep habits or eating habits)? *(circle YES or NO)*

YES   NO   Gotten a pamphlet for your child(ren) about it
YES   NO   Read an article or pamphlet yourself about it and then explained it to your child(ren)
YES   NO   Obtained or made a model to show about it
YES   NO   Taken your child(ren) to a lecture or film about it

52. Who in your family has had the responsibility for each of the following: *(write response)*

_____ Teaching the proper foods to eat
_____ Toilet training the child
_____ Teaching the child(ren) how to brush his/their teeth
_____ Buying medicines (prescriptions and nonprescriptions)
_____ Staying up with the child when he is ill
_____ Knowing what to do when the child is ill or injured
_____ Taking your child to the doctor or dentist

53. Who in the family has the responsibility for each of the following (male entirely, male somewhat more than female, both equally, female somewhat more than male, female entirely, neither male nor female):

male entirely	male somewhat more than female	both equally	female somewhat more than male	female entirely	neither male nor female	
0	1	2	3	4	5	Handling family finances
0	1	2	3	4	5	Deciding how to spend holidays
0	1	2	3	4	5	Religious matters
0	1	2	3	4	5	Choosing friends
0	1	2	3	4	5	Deciding how often to have sex
0	1	2	3	4	5	Deciding on the size of your family
0	1	2	3	4	5	Deciding on which method to use to prevent pregnancy

54. Please indicate whether you agree or disagree with each of the following statements:

AGREE   DISAGREE   Having "pull" is more important than ability in getting ahead
AGREE   DISAGREE   You should enjoy yourself while you can, because you never know what will happen tomorrow
AGREE   DISAGREE   A person has very little control over what happens to him
AGREE   DISAGREE   If you don't watch out people will take advantage of you
AGREE   DISAGREE   A person should look out after his own interests and let others do the same
AGREE   DISAGREE   Almost every week I see someone I dislike

55. Would you say that your health, in general, is

    EXCELLENT   GOOD   FAIR   POOR?   *(circle one)*

56. Do you have any additional comments on the questions we have asked?

    _____
    _____
    _____
    _____
    _____
    _____

57. If you know of any other men who have partially or entirely taken over household tasks, and who you think would be willing to participate in this research project, please give us their names and addresses:

    _____
    _____
    _____
    _____
    _____
    _____

THANK YOU VERY MUCH FOR YOUR COOPERATION

References

Aldous, D.
1974   "The Making of Family Roles and Family." *Family Coordinator*, July, 231 - 35.

Behrens, D.
1980   "His and Hers Housework." *Newsday*, 22 April, 4 - 6.

Bell, D.
1976   *The Cultural Contradictions of Capitalism.* New York: Basic Books.

Bem, W. Martyna, and C. Watson
1976   "Sex Typing and Adrogyny: Further Exploration of the Expressive Domain," *Journal of Personality and Social Psychology,* 34:1006 - 23.

Benson, L.
1968   *Fatherhood: A Sociological Perspective.* New York: Random House.

Benton and Bowles, Inc.
1980   *Men's Changing Role in the Family of the 80's: An American Consensus.*

Blood, R. and R. Hamblin
1958   "The Effect of the Wife's Employment on the Family Power Structure," *Social Forces,* 36:347 - 52.

Boston Women's Health Book Collective
1978   *Our Selves and Our Children.* New York: Random House.

Bronfenbrenner, U.
1960   "Freudian Theories of Identification and Their Derivatives," *Child Development,* 31:15 - 40.

Brozan, N.
1981 "A White House Report on Family Issues," *New York Times*, 23 October, C8.

Campbell, F.
1970 "Family Growth and Variation in the Family Role Structure," *Journal of Marriage and the Family*, 32:45 - 53.

Cunningham and Walsh, Inc.
1980 *Husbands as Homemakers.*

Fallding, H.
1961 "The Family and the Idea of the Cardinal Role," *Human Relations*, 14:329 - 50.

Fogarty, M., R. Rapoport; and R. Rapoport
1971 *Sex, Career and Family.* London: Allen & Unwin.

Freidson E.
1977 *The Professions and Their Prospects.* New York: Sage.

Geiken, K.
1964 "Expectations concerning Husband - Wife Responsibilities in the Home," *Journal of Marriage and the Family*, 26:349 - 52.

Goode, W.
1956 *Women in Divorce.* Glencoe: Free Press.

Grana, C.
1964 *Bohemian versus Bourgeois.* New York: Basic Books.

Hacker, H.
1957 "The New Burdens of Masculinity," *Marriage and Family Living*, 19:227 - 33.

Havighurst R., and A. Davis
1955 "A Comparison of the Chicago and Harvard Studies of Social Class Differences in Child Rearing," *American Sociological Review*, 20:438 - 42.

Heilbrun, A.
1965 "An Empirical Test of the Modeling Theory of Sex Role Learning," *Child Development*, 36:789 - 99.

Hoffman, L.
1960 "Effects of the Employment of Mothers on Parental Power Relations and the Division of Household Tasks," *Marriage and Family Living*, 22:27 - 35.

1961 "The Father's Role in the Family and the Child's Peer-Group Adjustment," *Merrill - Palmer Quarterly*, 7:97 - 105.

Hurwitz, N.
1960 "The Marital Roles Inventory and the Measurement of Marital Adjustment," *Psychological Reports*, 10:853 - 54.

Iglehart, A.
1979 "Housewives and Their Work, 1957 and 1976," paper presented at the 74th Annual Meeting of the American Sociological Association, Boston, Massachusetts; August.

Kiser, D.
1981 *Corpus Juris Secundum: A Complete Restatement of the Entire American Law*. American Law Book.

Klemesrud, J.
1981 "Two-Career Couples: Employers Listening," *New York Times*, 27 June, 21.

Komarovsky, M.
1967 *Blue Collar Marriage*. New York: Vintage.

1970 *Dilemmas of Masculinity*. New York: Norton.

Kuhn, M. and T. McPartland
1964 "An Empirical Investigation of Self-Attitudes," *American Sociological Review*, 19:68 - 76.

Kuhn, T.
1970 *The Structure of Scientific Revolutions*. Chicago: University of Chicago Press.

Lein, L.
1979 "Male Participation in Home Life: Impact of Social Supports and Breadwinner Responsibility on the Allocation of Tasks," *Family Coordinator*, 28:489 - 95.

Levine, J.
1975 *Who Will Raise the Children?* Boston: Lippincott.

Lopata, H.
1971 *Occupation: Housewife.* New York: Oxford University Press.

Lynn, D.
1973 "Sex Differences in Identification Development," N. Glazer, ed., *Woman in a Man-Made World*, Chicago: Rand McNally.

Mainardi, P.
1970 "The Politics of Housework," R. Morgan, ed., *Sisterhood Is Powerful.* New York: Random House.

McGrady, M.
1975 *The Kitchen Sink Papers: My Life as a Househusband.* New York: Doubleday.

Melsted, L.
1979 "Swedish Family Policy: Election Year '79." New York: Swedish Information Service.

Nelson, E.
1977 "Women's Work: Household Alienation," *Humboldt Journal of Social Science*, 5:1.

Newsweek
1981 "Commuting by Computer," 4 May, 58, 61.

Oakley, A.
1974 *The Sociology of Housework.* New York: Pantheon.

Parsons, T., and R. Bales, eds.
1955 *Family, Socialization and Interaction Process.* Glencoe: Free Press.

Pleck, J.
1977   "The Work - Family Role System," *Social Problems*, 24:417 - 26.

1979   "Men's Family Work: Three Perspectives and Some New Data," *The Family Coordinator*, October, 481 - 88.

Pratt, L.
1976   *Family Structure and Effective Health Behavior: The Energized Family.* Boston: Houghton Mifflin.

Presser, H.
1977   "Female Employment and the Division of Labor within the Home: A Longitudinal Perspective," paper presented at the Annual Meeting of the Population Association of America, St. Louis, Missouri, April.

Rapoport, R., and R. Rapoport
1976   *Dual Career Families Re-Examined.* London: Robertson.

Rau, L.
1960   "Parental Antecedents of Identification," *Merrill—Palmer Quarterly*, 6:77 - 82.

Reich, C.
1972   *The Greening of America.* New York: Bantam Books.

Robinson, James
1977   *Changes in Americans' Use of Time, 1965 - 1975.* Cleveland: Communications Research Center, Cleveland State University.

Robinson, Joan
1978   *An American Legal Almanac: Law in All States—A Summary and Update.* Dobbs Ferry, New York: Oceana.

Schechter, E.
1978   "Time Devoted to Housework and Its Division by Sex and Age: A Videotape Analysis," paper presented at the 77th Annual Meeting of the American Anthropological Association, Los Angeles, California, November.

Siefert, K.
1974 "Some Problems of Men in Child Care Center Work," Pleck and Sawyer, eds., *Men and Masculinity.* Englewood Cliffs, New Jersey: Prentice - Hall.

Sirjamaki, J.
1948 "Cultural Configurations in the American Family," *American Journal of Sociology,* 53:464- 70.

Stearns, P.
1980 *Be a Man!* New York: Holmes and Meier.

Stolz, L.
1960 "Effects of Maternal Employment on Children," *Child Development,* 31:749 - 82.

Sussman, M., and B. Cogswell
1972 "Variant Marriage Styles and Family Forms: Needed Theory and Research," paper presented at the 22nd Annual Meeting of the Society for the Study of Social Problems, New Orleans, Louisiana; August.

U.S. Bureau of the Census
1971, *Statistical Abstract of the United States.*
    1977

U.S. Department of Labor
1977 *Dictionary of Occupational Titles.* Washington, DC: U.S. Government Printing Office.

Vollmer, H., and D. Mills
1966 *Professionalization.* Englewood Cliffs: Prentice - Hall.

Walker, K.
1970 "Time Used by Husbands for Household Work," *Family Economics Review,* June, 8 - 11.

Walker, K., and M. Woods
1976 *Time Use: A Measure of Household Production of Goods and Services.* Washington, D.C.: American Home Economics Association.

148   HOUSEHUSBANDS

Weber, M.
1958   *The Protestant Ethic and the Spirit of Capitalism.* New York: Scribners.

Weil, M.
1961   "An Analysis of the Factors Influencing Married Women's Actual or Planned Work Participation," *American Sociological Review*, 26:91 - 96.

Widmer, K.
1977   "Reflections of a Male Housewife: On Being a Feminist Fellow-Traveler." C. Carney and S. McMahon, eds., *Exploring Contemporary Male/Female Roles.* La Jolla, Cal.: University Associates.

Work in America Institute
1980   "New Work Schedules for a Changing Society," New York: Work in America Institute.

Young, M., and P. Willmott
1973   *The Symmetrical Family.* New York: Pantheon.

Index

151